LOVE FOR
WE'VE GOT THIS

"In *We've Got This*, Ritu Bhasin teaches you how to embrace your uniqueness, unlock your power, and create an unshakable sense of belonging. This important book will help you tap into the courage and confidence to be your best self."

—MEL ROBBINS, *New York Times* bestselling author
and host of *The Mel Robbins Podcast*

"Having worked in the field of female empowerment for most of my life, I'm used to encouraging women at all levels to take their life, their careers, and their identity to the next level despite the obstacles in their way. Ritu Bhasin's inspirational *We've Got This* has helped me recognize the true power of community, of acceptance, of belonging in this fight. You are reading one woman's fight for identity, but the lessons she imparts are universal."

—DR. SHEFALI TSABARY, clinical psychologist
and *New York Times* bestselling author

"With *We've Got This*, Ritu Bhasin adds her powerful and influential voice to the critical discussion of how to heal in order to thrive, especially when it comes to experiencing belonging. Ritu's messages are needed more now than ever before."

—RESMAA MENAKEM, healer, trauma specialist, and *New York Times* bestselling author of *My Grandmother's Hands*

"With *We've Got This*, Ritu Bhasin lends her powerful voice to the empowerment space. Every lesson she shares is one that she's lived and earned. Growing up as a child of immigrants, feeling like an outsider, and achieving the 'corporate dream' only to realize it's not the key to happiness? These stories are familiar to so many of us, which is why Ritu's insights offer important lessons on how to thrive even in the face of painful experiences."

—SHELLEY ZALIS, CEO of The Female Quotient

"Not only is *We've Got This* a guiding light on the importance of authenticity and belonging, it's a practical guidebook on how to live your best life both personally and professionally—especially for people who constantly have hate coming their way. We need more of Ritu's inspiration!"

—MINDA HARTS, racial equity expert and bestselling author of *The Memo, Right Within,* and *You Are More Than Magic*

"*We've Got This* is a captivating and compelling read that outlines the path to standing in your power. Ritu's insightful messages and deeply personal stories about the trials and tribulations of finding belonging resonate with the passion and authenticity she's known for."

—JEFFREY REMEDIOS, Chairman and CEO, Universal Music Canada

"Ritu's passion for encouraging others to stand in their power leaps off the pages of *We've Got This*. Her knowledge of how to find belonging in the face of marginalization runs deep—as does her ability to move people to live their best by committing to change."

—VERNĀ MYERS, CEO of The Vernā Myers Company
and award-winning author of *Moving Diversity Forward*

"The world has so much to gain from hearing the stories of children of immigrants and their experiences with belonging, intergenerational trauma, and ongoing hardships. This is why *We've Got This* matters so much. Ritu's commitment to leading the revolution of healing and empowerment is inspiring."

—DR. SIMRAN JEET SINGH, inclusion consultant,
speaker, and bestselling author of *The Light We Give*

"*We've Got This* is the book many of us have been longing for: an inspiring road map for how to live and work more authentically to experience greater belonging. Ritu gives us hands-on, real-world guidance on how to be more of who we truly are, through the beautiful intwining of story, wisdom, and humor. But she also shines a powerful spotlight on the importance of bringing down the barriers to belonging for others and why we want to make this happen."

—DEEPA PURUSHOTHAMAN, DEI leader, speaker,
and bestselling author of *The First, the Few, the Only*

"*We've Got This* is the anthem we need now—an honest look at the source of our woundedness and a path to restoration that gives us a real shot at bringing our full selves to every space we occupy . . . and to each other."

—TARA JAYE FRANK, award-winning workplace
equity strategist and author of *The Waymakers*

ALSO BY RITU BHASIN

The Authenticity Principle: Resist Conformity, Embrace Differences, and Transform How You Live, Work, and Lead

RITU BHASIN

WE'VE GOT THIS

UNLOCKING THE BEAUTY OF
BELONGING

amplify
an imprint of Amplify Publishing Group

an imprint of Amplify Publishing Group

www.amplifypublishinggroup.com

We've Got This: Unlocking the Beauty of Belonging

For more information, please contact:
Amplify Publishing, an imprint of Amplify Publishing Group
620 Herndon Parkway, Suite 320
Herndon, VA 20170
info@amplifypublishing.com

Library of Congress Control Number: 2023900511

CPSIA Code: PRV0223A

ISBN-13: 978-1-63755-699-3

Printed in the United States

For Mama Bhasin, whose spirit encases me.

For Papa Bhasin, whose TLC lifts me.

For Sister Bhasin, whose presence is my anchor.

For Santosh, whose unwavering love is home.

And for everyone who longs to belong:
I see you, I feel you, and I'm here with you.

CONTENTS

CHAPTER ONE

UNLOCKING BELONGING

'm sitting cross-legged on top of my thin yoga mat in the main hall of the South Indian ashram. My eyes are closed, and my hands are on each knee in gyan mudra. The sun is fully out, but because a breeze is coming through the hall's open arched windows, the air is warm but tolerable, while the tiled floor is cool. Had I known we'd be sitting on the floor for hours each day, and that my butt would hate it this much, I would've paid the extra thirty bucks to bring a thicker mat with me.

We're meditating. Aside from the sounds of the wind rustling in the trees, the pesky bugs buzzing around, and the guy breathing heavily beside me, there's mostly silence in the room.

I'm supposed to be going deep within myself by tuning in to my breath. It's 2009 and I've told myself I must unlock inner peace and make myself one with the cosmos before I turn forty, which means I have six and a half years to do this. But, instead, I'm fussing in my mind about the yellow t-shirt and white pants I'm wearing—the uniform I was handed when I checked into the ashram for the four-week yoga teacher training program.

It's what the other few hundred yogis from around the world who are in the hall with me have on too.

I inhale. "If they expect us to wear this get-up every day, why only give us two sets?"

I exhale. "Why in the hell do they think white pants in a South Indian forest is a good idea?! Find me a woman who's good to wear white pants for twenty-eight days in a row."

Focus on your anahata chakra, Ritu.

Take your focus and your breath there.

You've got this.

Actually, I don't. "How am I going to handwash everything for two flipping months?!"

My mind floats to my Mom making ten-year-old me handwash the lacy doily things we use as coasters on the living room coffee table. They're extremely important because the furniture gods will zap you if you put any item directly on the wood. I'm despising every minute of hanging over the laundry room sink, while my Dad's voice in the background tells me, in Punjabi, to be gentle. My Bhua Ji (Dad's sister) made these, and my Dad transported them, with love, from India to Toronto when he first immigrated to the city.

Then I picture the brownish-burgundy pleather suitcases from our childhood.

Then my mind jumps to the expensive backpack I've brought with me on this solo adventure. As I think about how smug I felt walking into the ashram with it on, I tell myself the truth: I hate the thing. Its weight feels like it's going to break my back. And it makes me wonder why so many people enjoy camping, backpacking, portaging...

Come back.

Come back.

Come back to your breath.

Okay, okay. I'm back. I beam the light from my ajna into my anahata, which is what I think I'm supposed to be doing, and take some deep, cleansing breaths. "It's working, it's working. I'm finding stillness and peace."

But then my mind drifts to the thin mat under my butt. "Sometimes I can be so cheap. Why didn't I just buy the thicker mat?!"

"I'm not cheap!" I remind myself, "I spent four bazillion dollars on the backpack and that purse two months ago."

Good rebuttal.

Then why are you so worried about money all the time?!

My Dad's face pops into my head. He's wearing his favorite bright-red turban and grinning from ear to ear, showing off his perfect teeth, which he credits to the neem tree bark he used to chew on as a child growing up in India. I say hi to him quickly and then push myself to go back to connecting with my inner calm. I decide to use my go-to mantra to help me. "Satnam Waheguru, Satnam Waheguru, Satnam Waheguru."

I somehow manage to shut down the noise inside me for about seven breaths. Then it happens: the question I constantly grapple with in new situations pops into my mind.

"Who am I going to be while I'm here?"

Not this again.

Go back to breathing.

"No, seriously, who am I going to be? How do I fit in? What side do I show everyone?"

Change of plans.

These are good questions.

Let's stay with them for a bit.

"I could try to charm them with Corporate Ritu. I'll tell them about how I've taken a sabbatical from my law firm job to come here. And then I can slide in some details about the fancy work I do, the executive MBA I have coming up, and how proud my parents are of me..."

(Crickets.)

"Okay, how about I give them my sassy, thick-skinned, in-your-face, Badass Ritu?"

You're in a yoga ashram.

Really?

"Right. I'll explain how I'm here to study yoga but not actually become a teacher, and I'll give them super chill, mellow vibes?"

You?!

As if.

"Party Girl Ritu? Funny Pants Ritu? Sweet, Soft Ritu?"

Hmmm.

"Well, what do I show them then?!"

You know what to do.

"No, I don't."

Yes, you do.

Inhale. Exhale. Inhale. Exhale. "No, I really don't." And with that, the spiraling begins.

The reality is that I feel lost. I'm struggling with how to show up at the ashram because I don't know who I am anymore. After years of curating my image, I feel so disconnected from myself. And given what I went through as a child, I'm also plagued by intense feelings of unworthiness. Not only do I feel like I don't belong anywhere, I worry I'm only loved for what I do and not who I am. This is why I've created all these Ritu facades. The problem is, they're not healing my hurt.

And then there's my fixation with being happy-happy and perfect all the time. And with always wanting to achieve. I suppose this should be expected since I feel like both a success and a failure, especially in my parents' eyes. I don't know which one is more accurate, but it's like I'm trapped in a cage.

And with all the hateful messages that've come my way, I'm so confused about my cultural identities. Am I Canadian? Punjabi? Indian? South Asian? Sikh? A Brown girl? A citizen of the world? "Who the hell am I?!" loops nonstop in my head.

And it's not just that I don't know who I am or feel like I don't belong anywhere, I can't stand the life I've created for myself. As I sit here on the ashram floor, I can't help but think about how much I hate my job, my main friend crew, and the grip my parents have on me. Plus, I feel so ashamed about being in my early thirties with no boyfriend prospects in sight, fully aware of my plummeting value on the Indian bride market—not that I've dated a Brown guy since I was fifteen anyway.

This is so much.

Too much.

And I find it perplexing that I both loved the book *Eat, Pray, Love* and instantly feel enraged when people immediately exclaim, "Like *Eat, Pray, Love*?" when I tell them I'm going back to *my* motherland to study an ancient way of life from *my* culture. I also worry the other yogis will think I'm an angry, radical activist type if I open up about how sick I am of how oppression—and especially white supremacy and patriarchy, including their intersection—permeates every aspect of our global society, even here in this South Indian ashram where it seems White men are running it. On top of which, the concept of a yoga teacher's certificate is a colonial construct, which makes me question why, if I know this, I even chose to come here in the first place.

Pause, girl.

I wish I could escape my life.

Really, stop.

Take some deep breaths.

It's in that precise moment that it dawns on me why they gave us the yellow t-shirt and white pants to wear.

THE PATH TO BELONGING

The path to belonging is beautiful.

The path to belonging is hard.

Both are true.

And it serves us to hold both truths at once.

Because experiencing belonging isn't a smooth, straight path for many of us; it's a ride along a winding road that's filled with highs and lows and peaks and bumps. But once we've felt the beauty of belonging, we know how important it is.

Belonging is the profound feeling of being accepted and honored for who you are, especially for what makes you different, by your own self and by the people you choose to be bonded with. It's about fulfilling your instinctive human need to be affirmed for your authenticity. To belong, first and foremost, you must know, embrace, and be who you are deep inside you. Simply put, you must experience belonging with yourself. This is what will empower you to claim the belonging you deserve with others. They must receive and accept you for your true self.

And here's another critical point: belonging isn't a "nice to have," it's a "must have" to feel safe, healthy, and joyful. As humans, it's part of our survival. We *long* for belonging. We're wired to crave acceptance in intimate relationships and interactions with others, whether this is with our elders, siblings, relatives, lovers, friends, leaders, teammates, or classmates, and even random strangers. We both need and want to be seen and respected for who we are across all our identities.

But we also want to feel connected to a greater whole. We deeply desire being part of a community or communities. We want union with others that's rooted in shared purpose, meaning, and respect. But this can never be at the expense of being who we are. Belonging with others only happens when we're being embraced for our authenticity, particularly our differences.

> " Belonging is the profound feeling of being accepted and honored for who you are, especially for what makes you different, by your own self and by the people you choose to be bonded with.

This is why when you experience belonging, it feels glorious. Your body and mind let you know you're feeling safe and at ease, so you can relax, melt into the moment, and be yourself. Your soul swells with love, warmth, and gratitude because you're being seen. You burst with radiant light and you come alive— because belonging is *beautiful*.

It's also why the inverse is true: when you feel unwanted, both by your own self and by others, it can feel heartbreaking. Your body will reveal it's holding fear, hurt, and loneliness. Your spirit will struggle—because being rejected is *hard*.

In my early thirties, I was just beginning to understand how my bumpy, curvy path to belonging was filling my life with angst. Up until then, given all I'd been through, I was consistently behaving as what I call my "Performing Self"—which, in my book *The Authenticity Principle*, I define as the self you show up as when you feel like you don't have a choice but to conform or hide who you are because otherwise you believe people will reject, hate, or judge you.

Both knowingly and unknowingly, you use your Performing Self as a mask to cloak the pain that lives inside you *and* to protect you from the hurt that comes from being othered—which is what happens when others treat you poorly or reject you because you don't behave how they want you to. It's like life is a giant stage and we're actors putting out our best theatre: we bury who we actually want to love, we stay in relationships that don't honor us, we take on jobs we hate, we hold back in giving our opinions, we contort our voices and accents, we dress in ways we don't want to, and so much more. But the pressure to be someone we're not hurts our soul. It strikes at our ability to belong *and* it smothers our spark—the powerful flame of greatness that lives inside all of us.

When I reached the ashram, I thought I needed my Performing Self to shield myself from others' scrutiny, feel less messed up, and attract love. I was performing across all areas of my life, but the most insidious way was probably my fixation on constantly being positive, perfect, and in achievement mode. If I could keep projecting sunshine, getting a ten out of ten on everything I did, and winning accolades, then maybe I'd finally belong. I learned to act out positivity-perfection-achievement so well that it became a special part of my Performing Self—I might as well have tattooed "PPA" on my chest.

In fact, I'd become so used to "acting" Ritu instead of *being* Ritu, I didn't know who I was. And this is why I didn't know how to take my Performing Self mask off when I first got to the ashram. Stripped of my personas by the yellow t-shirt and white pants, I had no idea of which "Ritu" signaled the most positivity-perfection-achievement, who I could then use to gain acceptance.

But that's not all. As I sat on the ashram floor, reeling from the realization I was struggling to find belonging and joy in life, I was also startled by how hard life was. Up to this point, I thought life was only supposed to be beautiful. I wasn't expecting unending curves and bumps. No one had ever sat me down and said:

> Listen, my beloved Ritu, life is a blessing. But it can also be really tough, especially when you feel you don't belong. You'll deal with all kinds of rejection and oppressive garbage. You'll feel confused about how you were raised. You'll rail against and resist who you are. You'll feel like a yo-yo because of how people treat you, and your heart will hurt from often breaking. And, my darling Brown girl born of working-class immigrant Punjabi Sikh parents, there will also be lots of hate. The thing is, life isn't a magical path of nonstop happiness, nor is happiness a permanent state. Instead,

happiness is about experiencing as many moments of joy as possible by finding belonging as your true self. Fear not though, you're going to develop incredible wisdom that'll help you to understand and make this happen. Keep working on healing, anchoring to who you are, and focusing on the fiery spark that's inside you. This'll lead you to release your greatness into the world. Finally, Sweet, Soft Ritu, your life will also be filled with beautiful belonging. And you're worthy of it.

This was the "someone should've told me" letter I desperately needed from my childhood into my thirties. I got bits and pieces of it over time, but it took a three-month sabbatical from work, going halfway around the world, and donning a uniform to get to a place where I could give myself this message. Being pushed to spend hours, days, and weeks on deeply connecting with myself was the catalyst I needed for transformation. It unlocked a cascade of life-altering lessons and experiences that carried on for years.

And this is what ultimately led me to take off so much of my Performing Self mask and my PPA armor and replace them with what I call *core wisdom*.

Core wisdom is the knowing you hold within you that helps you to rise above, heal from, and protect against the hurtful things coming your way that strike at your ability to belong. Your core wisdom pushes you to tune in to and care for your body and mind, tend to your wounds, interrupt negative self-talk, become more resilient, connect to who you are, stand in your power, speak your truth, and so much more. This knowing becomes a faithful anchor in your life, which you then rely on for every decision you make going forward. It's what'll help you to recognize you're experiencing belonging and identify how to create more of these moments, including by drawing on the practices I'll share with you in these pages.

It's my core wisdom that helped me to finally understand the power of choice—that I can choose to shift my mindset, behavior, and actions to live a better life. My core wisdom has moved me from constantly feeling unlovable to feeling beautiful about my authentic self. My core wisdom has led me to embrace the mix of identities that make up who I am instead of putting myself into a box. It's guided me to finally let go of most of the pressure to project perma-positivity when I don't feel that way. It's pushed me to make a dent in my need to be perfect. And it's even helped me to chip away at my fixation on achievement.

My core wisdom is carrying me along the up-and-down path of life, and I want it to do the same for you. While it can take a lot of hard work to feel its magic, the core wisdom you'll develop through the takeaways and practices in this book will help you to live your best life and not just cope during your time on this planet. You don't need to spend weeks at an ashram or wear anything yellow to heal from the hurtful experiences that come your way. Instead, you can do this anywhere, and the small steps you immediately take to grow your core wisdom will help you experience greater belonging along your life's journey.

This is what I want for you. And I know you've got this.

OUR JOURNEY AHEAD

As the eldest daughter born into a Punjabi immigrant-run household, I was assigned a role that's automatically given in my culture to those who are blessed to be the first child: the second mom or third parent. Given that I came into this world already very bossy and assertive, I happily took on the esteemed role, much to my sister's and brother's horror. I don't blame them. It's an obnoxious combo and one that's repeatedly bitten me in the tail.

Technically, I also got the title "Bhenji," which basically means respected sister and is mostly used by younger siblings with their elder sisters. I say technically only because, in moving to Canada, my parents wanted to be "modern" immigrants. Much to my disappointment, they said "nope" to using traditional titles within our family, so my sister and brother have never called me Bhenji.

But it doesn't matter. Because, in my heart, I'm Bhenji to them and to everyone else on this planet and always will be. I was born to be Ritu Bhenji, because all I've ever wanted is the opportunity to provide my advice to anyone who might need it. Telling people what to do? I'm on it, and I do it well. Want my feedback? Prepare yourself for a three-hour monologue. Don't want my feedback? All good, I may give it to you anyway.

It won't be shocking then to hear me say I've designed a career for myself where I get paid to be Ritu Bhenji for a living. I've now presented to hundreds of thousands of people around the world, and I've coached over a thousand professionals. Through my work, I've had a front-row seat to understanding why some people get ahead, why others don't, what the barriers are, and what to do about it. Given my struggle to belong, these experiences have helped me, but they've also offered up lots of thoughts that the Bhenji in me wants to impart. And that is why I wrote this book.

In these pages, I share what I've learned about hurting, healing, and belonging, for anyone who's felt othered but who now wants to come alive, rise, and thrive. For your journey ahead, I'm going to flag important lessons, takeaways, and reflection questions to help you unlock limitless experiences of belonging in your life, even in difficult moments.

- In *Hurting*, I'll talk about what causes us to feel unlovable and like we don't belong, and why it's important to reflect on what happened to you as a child to better understand why and how you're showing up now as an adult.
- In *Healing*, I'll dig into the incredible power of using core wisdom to release the pain you're holding, embrace who you are, and become more resilient, so that you become more settled and joyful.
- In *Belonging*, I'll take you through how you can tap into your authenticity, stand in your power, use your voice, experience greater acceptance, and live your best.

Much of this work is tough to do. It has been for me. It's highlighted the hardest relationship to navigate: the one I have with myself. It's meant exploring the impact of being vilified by others. It's revealed that facing oppression makes a hard life even harder. Not to mention, it's taken unyielding commitment, vulnerability, self-compassion, and patience.

Given all of this, I get why some of us don't want to do this work. But my deep hope is that, because you're looking to heal and shine, you *will* do it. I want you to unravel the beliefs you're holding that lead you to feel like you're inferior, unworthy, and unlovable, and replace these negative narratives with the truth, which is that you are intelligent, beautiful, remarkable, resilient, competent, accomplished, loving, kind, and creative.

I want you to uncover and unleash the greatness that you already embody and hold within you. I'm about you being you—your best, healthiest, and most anchored you—and radiating that light in all that you do. I want you to step into your power in every moment so that you can feel in your bones you are revolutionary.

This is my hope for you.

$$\equiv$$

When I was young, and in the thick of feeling despair from all the darkness I was experiencing, if you'd asked me if I knew that one day I'd grow up to be a fiery lioness, I would've looked at you blankly and then gone back to reading my thesaurus, which I did for fun back then.

If you'd shared with me that, as part of my journey to claim belonging, I'd learn to love myself, my identities, my personality, and my body, I wouldn't have accepted this as the truth.

If you'd explained to me that after years of feeling ugly, I'd finally start to feel beautiful in my skin, both inside and out, I would've rejected that.

If you'd told me that my mere presence is revolutionary given all the barriers that I've overcome and continue to be in my way, the significance of this would've gone over my head.

But if you'd let me know that when I was older, I'd commit my life to working hard to both heal my pain and bring down hate, I *would've* believed you. Because, somewhere deep down within me, I always knew how I was being treated was wrong. All the loathing, isolation, and disrespect—I knew it was unjust. A tiny spark inside me told me I deserved better. And it also said, "So does everyone else who's been hurting just like you."

And this is why belonging matters.

Whether it's a slower process of growing your core wisdom or a dramatic shift that fundamentally moves you to change the way you're living, what's most important is you choose to live life differently so that you can heal. *And* thrive. *And* be anchored to your authentic self, feel gorgeous inside and out, build an amazing community of beloveds around you, and, in the end, have more moments of joy. This is what belonging is all about.

And I'm excited and filled with hope about what lies ahead for our growing community. This moment in time can be a massive turning point. We can choose to reframe how we look at our beautiful, wild, difficult, and unpredictable journey to claiming belonging, especially when hurtful stuff continues to come at us. We can choose to re-commit to falling in love with ourselves and to experiencing belonging as much as possible. We can choose to bring this spirit into how we treat others. We can choose to be there for each other when we need it most.

Ultimately, my hope is that my story deeply resonates with you. And I have a feeling it will. I say this because I know in my heart that *my* story is *your* story. It's the human story of desiring belonging.

I've got this.

You've got this.

We've got this.

HURTING

CHAPTER TWO

OUR STORIES BEGAN LONG AGO

I hear their voices as I slowly tiptoe down the hallway of our small house toward their bedroom. Gingerly poking my head into the doorway, I see both of them at once. To my little body, they look so grand.

My mother stands in front of the mirror, a cream-colored sari blouse and petticoat covering most of her slim, but curvy, figure. She's now humming to herself as she combs her thick, jet-black hair, which falls well below her waist. With every stroke, her head moves ever so slightly, causing her thick mane to rhythmically swish from side to side. She starts to accessorize her body and delicately slips 22-karat gold bangles onto her tiny wrists—bracelets that were given to her by my Nani (her mom) on a recent trip back home to India.

She looks like a queen. I want to be absorbed into her light.

I look past her to my remarkably handsome father. He's wearing just a white undershirt and black pants as he quietly navigates an iron across the delicate fabric of the off-white and peacock-blue sari my mother will drape over her enviable curves—yards and yards of shiny, gorgeous silk. I'm captivated by how he moves. He's always so careful and meticulous, whether it's sitting at the sewing machine to stitch new curtains or towering over the hot stove to cook up chicken curry and mattar paneer. At my tender age of six, I have no idea I'm being raised in a dynamic household that's a mix of progressive and traditional norms, though I will learn over time.

My father hasn't put a turban on yet, so I can still see his long, unshorn hair tied neatly into a big bun atop his head. He'll likely choose a red or maroon one from his collection, but before he does, he'll ask me which one I like the best. Helping him to match turbans to outfits will become a practice we'll do together for decades to come—and I'll love every minute of it.

With his crown-like turban on his head, he's a king in my eyes.

Together, they'll turn heads at the family party tonight, as they always do. As tall, beautiful, striking people, they both admit they gave the go-ahead to their arranged marriage based on their shared good looks. Down the road, my siblings and I will often hear from others that we've won the gene pool lottery, something I'll struggle to take in given that it's not how I've come to see myself. But as I stand there watching them in my pink tailor-made-in-India frock ironed by my father, with white satin ribbons laced into my braids by my mother, I have no awareness of any of this. I'm just taking in my superheroes—regal beings I'm both infatuated with and petrified of.

My mother looks up as she closes the clasp on her necklace, catching me hovering in the doorway.

"Hi, my Putri!" she says, a smile stretching across her face. "You look so pretty. Now, go put your socks on."

My *Putri*. I love when they call me that. It essentially means "my beloved daughter" in Punjabi, and it's a word that's used to convey love, affection, and fondness.

Every time I hear this word, it's like my heart is going to burst. I feel loved and wanted and adored. I feel like I matter. And so, I never tire of hearing it. Not as a teenager, even during all our struggles and the conflict. Not in my twenties, when I feel pressure to live the life they want me to lead. Not in my thirties, when I try to interrupt our codependence by drawing boundaries. And especially not in my forties, when I realize a time is coming very soon when I'll only hear this word in my memories.

≡

Our life stories begin with our elders' life stories. I say elders because it wasn't just our parents who raised us. Many of us have an army of elders who've influenced us: our grandparents, aunts, uncles, siblings and cousins, and people we aren't related to by blood but who we call family, because they are. We're shaped by their values, personalities, hobbies, and frankly, almost every aspect of who they are—which directly connects with what we learned about how to belong.

In fact, here's a profound takeaway: our elders' experiences with belonging become threads that are woven into the fabric of our beings. Both directly and indirectly, what happens to them in their pursuit to belong becomes part of us—from the parenting messages they absorbed to the energy around them to the genetics they inherited, we're touched by every aspect of their stories. This impact is why it's important to dig deep into our family roots. We want to learn about the imprint their paths to belonging have had on us—something we're able to better understand when we pause to reflect on this as adults.

> This chapter opens the door to exploring how our hurting begins and shares a bit of my family history to inspire you to reflect on the impact your elders' stories with belonging have had on you.

WHERE OUR THREADS OF BELONGING BEGIN

In my twenties and thirties, I knew my life was entwined with what my parents had gone through. But it wasn't until I started to study trauma that I began to understand how deeply their struggles to find belonging affected me.

My parents' journey began in the land then known as India, where they were both born in the 1940s. This was a huge moment in history because the British had finally agreed to give up formal control of the region after hundreds of years

17

of domination in various forms—a period marked by unspeakable horrors done to our people, lands, resources, systems, and practices.

When the British finally ended their official reign, they left behind a horrific aftermath. This included the impact of their "strategic help" in carving up the region into Hindu-majority India and Muslim-majority Pakistan, which at the time included Bangladesh, in such a way they knew would create havoc, because they were devastated to see their "jewel in the crown" colony go. Many South Asians call this moment in time "Partition," a term that's now synonymous with the pain resulting from the ethnic and religious bloodbaths, the creation of millions of displaced peoples, and a whole host of other issues.

> " Our elders' experiences with belonging become threads that are woven into the fabric of our beings. Both directly and indirectly, what happens to them in their pursuit to belong becomes part of us.

My Mama was just a baby when my grandparents, as Sikhs, made the difficult decision to abandon their lives in an area that is now part of Pakistan and flee to Delhi to protect themselves from the bloodshed. As part of exiling, they literally escaped with the shirts on their backs, little kiddies in tow. My Dad's family had been pushed to make this life-changing move a few years prior, before the carnage started.

It's so hard for me to wrap my mind around what my parents, grandparents, great-grandparents, and great-great-grandparents went through with colonialism and its impact on them. But I can tell you this: in my body now lives the trauma directly connected to my ancestors' experiences. I can feel the hurt pulse through my body when I reflect on the lost lives, flagrant violence, abused souls, rampant poverty, stunted prosperity, blatant theft, depleted resources, and co-opted traditions, relating to the oppression they faced.

Sometimes I think about where India would be right now if it hadn't been colonized: How would we be thriving right now? What would our art look like? How would our ancient healing practices be making the world a better place? What else would we have invented? What would belonging look like in our culture?

I think about my family tree. Given all the hurt and pain that's been passed along generation after generation, how much healthier would we be right now? How much more belonging would we be experiencing?

My mind also wanders to the pieces of my family history that've been taken from us. I'm picturing the nose ring my great-grandmother wore on her wedding day that I could've worn on mine. Or the sword my great-grandfather used to fight the British that I could've run my fingers across to remind myself that I have warrior blood in my veins. Or photos of ancestors I look like that I could've used growing up to rebut my siblings' assertion I was swapped at birth.

Stolen. Lost. Gone.

Growing up, my elders rarely, if ever, talked about Partition and the impact it had on their lives. Here and there, my Dad would beam with pride as he recalled the revolutionary spirit of the Sikhs in resisting and fighting the British, but that was about it. When I would directly ask about it, I'd get a variation of "Why are you bringing up those old memories, we don't need to talk about those things!" or "I don't remember."

It's only in their senior years that I've had a few more revealing glimpses into their memories. And one of them was uniquely startling.

≡

It's a Sunday afternoon, and I'm visiting Mama Bhasin and Papa Bhasin (what I affectionately call my parents) with Santosh, the love of my life. Over the years Santosh and I have been together, we've developed a pleasant routine for our weekend visits with them: tea at the kitchen table to start, a walk out-doors to follow, and then a yummy homecooked Punjabi meal made by my parents—enough for a hefty doggy bag.

As I sit at the kitchen table with my Dad, I can see a mix of red, auburn, and yellow leaves on the trees in the backyard. We're a few months away from having our worlds shut down because of the pandemic, but, in this moment, we have no idea of the chaos that's to come.

I stare at Papa Bhasin as he's going on and on in his fine chatty fashion, thinking to myself, "This is why I don't ever shut the frog up." At the same time, I can hear

Mama Bhasin's singsong voice from the other room as she laughs with Santosh. She adores him and is so happy that I've finally meshed my life with "my person," even though I'm in my early forties and I'm old as dirt by Indian norms.

I look down at my teacup as I try to land on how to interrupt my father's *multiple* trains of thought. I've come for the visit today with an objective. I'm in the midst of completing my trauma professional certification, and I want to steer him in the direction of what I just learned in class: that exile is one of the most difficult events the body can experience and it can cause trauma, which we then hold inside us. I've also been grappling with what I'm uncovering about the genetic inheritance and intergenerational transference of trauma. I'm starting to have a mind-blowing realization about the pain that lives inside me: my trauma isn't just about what's happened to me. It's directly linked to the hurt my parents have been carrying since they were born.

I wish I could ask my Mom about her memories, since it was her family that actually escaped in the midst of the Partition bloodshed. My cousin has shared with me that her father (my uncle and my Mom's elder brother) sometimes wakes up in the middle of the night screaming, "They're coming to get us, they're coming to get us." I can't imagine the memories that trigger his cries at night. But we're still in the early stages of my Mom's Alzheimer's diagnosis, so I'm not sure if she'll be able to talk about this, and I don't want to upset her in this already delicate moment. Instead my plan is to pepper my Dad with questions.

As he dips his rusk into his cha, he pauses to take a breath. I've found my opening. Immediately jumping on the two seconds of silence, I blurt out, "Dadda, can I change the subject?"

Without giving him a chance to respond, I launch into a brief overview of what we've been studying in my program and, in particular, what we just learned about the link between trauma, conflict, and exile. I then say to him, "I wanted to ask you, do you remember Partition?"

Without any shift or movement in his face or body, he responds in English, in his awesome Punjabi-influenced accent: "Yes, I do."

"What do you remember?" I ask.

"The fighting."

My heart starts to beat a bit faster. "Like, you'd hear about it?"

"No, I saw it," he says in a matter-of-fact tone. "I'd watch it in front of the house."

I want to make sure I have it right: "You saw people fighting in front of your house?"

"Yes, I saw people fighting, being killed," he casually answers.

The blood starts to drain from my face. Telling myself to be calm, I ask in a voice about five octaves higher, "What did you see?"

"I saw mobs killing Muslims."

I'm stunned. Especially given all of what I'm learning in the program right now. Managing to find some words, I ask, "How old were you?"

"Oh, I don't know! Why so many questions?!" He rolls his eyes. "We don't need to talk about this."

I know I should stop because he clearly wants to, but I can't bring myself to just yet. "Just one more question, Dadda. How old were you?"

"I don't know." He sighs. "Maybe five?"

Not wanting to push any further, I softly say, "I'm so sorry to hear this. It's so sad. It must've been so awful to see all this." I pause and take a big breath. "Maybe we can talk some more about this another time?"

"You don't have to ask me again—you can Google it," he replies.

And with that, he immediately goes back to his laundry list of critiques he has about the new family that's just moved in a few houses down.

=

I've reflected a lot on that conversation with my father and similar ones with him and others. I've come to believe that it's not that our elders don't care or are uninterested in talking to us about what happened in their pasts, whether it's the pain relating to life struggles, colonialism, or other oppression. It's that our elders do care, and they would share if they could, but it hurts them to talk about what happened back home. It's too much to let out the depth of the anguish of what they went through. Like so many of us when it comes to deeply painful experiences, they're walled up or they're numb or detached from what happened as coping mechanisms to manage their upset and their trauma.

This hurt is why so many of us tiptoe around digging into our elders' stories—we don't want to trigger them, and we want to honor their boundaries. But we know their pain runs deep, because we can feel it in them. And we know that it's affected their path to belonging.

My parents' journey as a married couple started in the early 1970s in Canada. In trying to leave their pain and trauma back home, I can't imagine how grueling it was for my parents, and any other immigrants who had similar experiences, to come to a country that screamed, "Sure, we'll take you for your labor, but you don't belong." A country where they barely knew anyone and making friends wasn't easy; where the grocery stores didn't carry the right ingredients to make their native dishes; where they spoke the official language in a way that was mocked; where their indigenous clothing made them a target for public ridicule; where their spirituality was demonized when they engaged in it; and where they were relentlessly pushed to put on a Performing Self mask and positivity-perfection-achievement armor to cloak their authenticity.

And this is on top of the financial strain they experienced: from the invalidation of their educational credentials to nonstop rejection for jobs they were overqualified for, to being underpaid for superior work, to needing to work multiple jobs at once, to putting food on the table for us while sending money back home to put food on tables there too, it was so hard for our elders to relax about finances. And we, as their kids, often felt the pressure through the constant stress buzzing in the background of our lives.

As long-haired, curry-eating, Punjabi suit-wearing, brown-skinned Sikh (decolonization moment: it's pronounced Sickh and not Seek) immigrants with thick Indian accents and not a lot of money, my parents stuck out, which meant endless harassment and subpar treatment. At every turn, they struggled emotionally and financially, as many immigrants do when they move to a country where they don't look or act like the majority.

"It was worth it because we knew we'd build a better life for our family" is what most elders say, mine included, when we ask about the hardships they've faced as immigrants. They wanted to ensure that we, as their children, would have a good life, a better life than they had.

And here's where the complicated world of life being both beautiful and hard comes in.

Many of us did have upbringings that were marked by beauty, goodness, levity, and security. I'm thinking about all the loving moments where my elders did less, ate less, and bought less for themselves so that we could do more, eat more, and have more. I'm reminiscing about the kisses and the hugs and the cuddles and the "I love yous" even when they were scrape-me-off-the-floor exhausted. I'm remembering the special occasions where they'd stretch what they could afford so that we could go on a class trip or get the new shoes the other kids had. I'm also reflecting on all the ways—affordable ways, of course—in which they went out of their way to create fun for us: picnics, road trips, religious gatherings, cousin sleepovers, and family parties.

Oh, but the family party in particular! Picture a classic family party with 150 of your closest "aunties," "uncles," and "cousins" crammed into the backyard, garage, basement, and/or living room, sitting on furniture wrapped in plastic—all while taking in the smell of food being cooked in massive steel pots on camping stoves outdoors, so that the spices wouldn't stink up the lacy beige curtains. Visualize the tables covered in delicious, piping-hot food served up in silver-foil trays or CorningWare baking dishes with either a blue flower or a yellow-red-brown vegetable pattern. Recall the music from back home blaring out of speakers as multiple generations danced together on the makeshift dance floor: the cute kiddies, the too-cool-for-school teens and young adults, the hot aunties in their fabulous custom-made outfits, and the drunken uncles with their hysterical dancing. Imagine all the late-night singing where the elders would break into song, taking turns belting out tunes they grew up on, while everyone else chimed in.

Whatever our cultural backgrounds are, many of us can remember great times and loving moments during our upbringings. For all of this, we can express gratitude and take in the feelings of love and warmth and joy that come up for us. It's healing.

But at the same time, we can also confess that we went through a lot of hard times, stress, and heaviness.

HURT PEOPLE HURT PEOPLE

Many of us grappled with difficult life experiences like loss and grief, relationship issues, toxic relatives, family conflict, and more. But many of us also struggled with the difficulties related to the pain our elders internalized back home, plus the hurt they encountered in their new homelands because they didn't feel like they belonged. As their kids, we felt vicarious sorrow. We may not have been able to put our finger on this while growing up—I can only see this now as an adult—but life was really hard for them *and* for us.

Many of our elders who are women, our mothers specifically, bore the brunt of the pain and hardships in our families because of the sting of oppression, including the reinforcement of binary gender norms and identities and intersectional inequities. On top of everything else, how they managed to run our households while working, often multiple jobs, and caring for young kiddies, with next to no childcare support, boggles my mind! I could go on and on for days and days about this. So let's shout it out: women, and especially immigrant women, are remarkable in so many ways.

But I also want to pause for a moment on our fathers, grandfathers, uncles, brothers, and cousins and their experiences with life's barriers and challenges. We don't talk about their stories as much, and it's only during intimate moments that I'll hear stories about how the journey to belong was so hard for them too. I think about all the smart, strong, vibrant, beautiful men out there—like my six-foot-two, red-turban-wearing father—who, despite their excellence, were held back from shining because they too felt the pressure to put on a Performing Self mask and PPA armor. I wonder how much better our world would be right now if they'd been able to live out their fullest potential, and I wonder how much healthier and happier each of us would be right now too.

I'm highlighting our health and happiness as their children for a reason. Because of toxic masculinity, and its intersection with other forms of oppression, many of our elders who are men felt pushed to be "manly" and to maintain an air of bravado, which meant acting "strong" and dominant and in control, even in the face of experiencing pain and humiliation. They could be angry and vent and rage, but many of them didn't know how to share their pain, sadness, and grief about being othered, nor did they feel safe to explore how this was impacting their mental health.

But repressing these feelings didn't mean they went away. Instead, for some of them, these emotions turned into self-hate, frustration, and despair, which they then let loose at home.

I both feel this and hear about this all the time in the stories people share with me. And it's heartbreaking.

$$\equiv$$

I'm at a big conference where I presented on the importance of authentic living a few hours earlier, and I've just finished the book signing event. *The Authenticity Principle* has been out for a while now, but I'm still pinching myself. The little girl in me who was haunted by bullies never would've imagined that people would line up to buy her book, let alone want her to sign it.

It's at events like these that I meet so many incredible spirits and I'm reminded that there's a huge community of us out there—all wanting to heal, love, help, and belong. It fills me with so much hope.

As I start to get up from the table, from the corner of my eye I see a man hovering at the side of the room. I turn my head fully in his direction and wave at him. He smiles shyly and slowly makes his way over. After introducing himself, he says to me, "As I listened to you talk about both how hard *and* rewarding it is to find belonging, I kept thinking, 'How does she know my life story?!' I felt like I was the only one in the room and you were talking to my heart."

He then reveals he immigrated to the U.S. as a child and tells me a bit about his upbringing. His father was a successful engineer back home, but his parents moved their family to America when the kids were young to escape the war that was happening in their homeland. Upon settling, his father couldn't find an engineering job because his degrees weren't recognized, and since they couldn't afford to have him re-qualify, he took odd jobs, finally ending up at a factory and eventually becoming a supervisor there.

Eyes watering, he continues, "My dad is so creative. He was an artist, but he had to give that up. He wanted to invent things, but he gave that up too. He never complains, but he always seems so sad and defeated."

It's not the first time I've heard these words. As he speaks, my mind keeps drifting to other stories people have told me about their families.

Like my friend who shared that her grandpa was such a happy man. He'd laugh and joke over breakfast, but then he'd go out into the world, and at least a few times a month, he'd come home withdrawn and distant. He'd tell the family about how he was being humiliated at work, and then grab a bottle, drink until he passed out, and be zoned out for days. It was so hard on the whole family, but on her grandma and mom especially.

Or the message I got online from someone who confided that her dad was constantly filled with rage about how hard life was for him. She told me that her family could tell that he was so stressed all the time, although he'd never say this outright. Instead, he'd lash out at them.

As I look into the eyes of the gentle-souled man standing in front of me, I feel his pain—the same way I have when others have shared their stories and when I think of my own.

He takes a breath and then tells me, "My father says he's living through us, his kids. I just can't get it out of my head that he never got to live out his dreams. Imagine all the ways in which he could've helped the world? Or been happier? Or been less broken?"

He pauses for a moment, looks away, and then adds, "Or all of the ways I'd be less broken right now?"

Imagine, indeed.

≡

I weep for all the men out there who wanted to do better and to belong but didn't know how to make this happen, who didn't have the tools to heal, and who didn't feel safe to reveal what was really happening inside them.

Let me be clear, I'm not excusing abusive, toxic behavior. We each own our actions, and we're each responsible for doing good and for minimizing harm in all we do. Instead, I want to draw attention to how challenging and nuanced and difficult it can be to explore the impact of pain and trauma on our lives. I'm highlighting how so much of what we're going through is intergenerational: so many of our ancestors had hurt and harm done upon them by colonizers, by other oppressors, and by their own family members. From these experiences, they learned how to hurt and harm, and, in turn, they passed this along from generation to generation—because hurt people hurt people.

Again, we're responsible for our own actions, which includes interrupting cycles of hurt and harm. We must hold ourselves and each other accountable for this. But it's also important that we see this as a collective experience. In fact, this is a big takeaway for us all: there are patterns of behavior in our communities that are responses to what happened to us over generations. This isn't an excuse but a deeper appreciation of what we've experienced in our communities and a reinforcement of why we need to break these cycles and commit to healing.

> " Many of our ancestors had hurt and harm done upon them by colonizers, by other oppressors, and by their own family members. From these experiences, they learned how to hurt and harm, and, in turn, they passed this along from generation to generation—because hurt people hurt people.

It also speaks to why, across the different experiences we had, so many of us are filled with a complicated mashup of emotions when we think about our elders. With one breath, we feel love, gratitude, pride, and tenderness. With the next breath, we feel anger, irritation, resentment, and upset. With the following breath, we feel guilt, duty, sadness, and heartbreak. And then with all the other breaths we take, there are the feelings of shame, fatigue, and confusion about how to be authentic in their presence. Not to mention, it can take our breath away entirely when we pause to reflect on this kernel of truth: since they weren't able to claim belonging for themselves, how were they going to teach and model for us how to make this happen for ourselves?

It can be very confusing to make sense of this cocktail of feelings and even harder to reconcile them all. We'll get to work on that soon when I explore the power of core wisdom, but for now, I want to go back to what I said earlier about not viewing life and belonging in binary ways and share this insight: you can hold all of these emotions about your elders at once.

As you work on your own healing, you can use your core wisdom to make sense of the mashup. You may never be rid of the complicated mix, but that's not what's important. What matters is that you can be at peace with knowing you can hold complex feelings about your elders while increasingly seeing them as people who are on their own journeys to find belonging.

I can tell you that the awareness, empathy, and compassion I now hold for my parents, given all they went through, has not only led me to love them even more intensely, but it has helped me on my own path to heal my wounds and to experience greater belonging. And if I can be tender, loving, kind, and understanding about the good, bad, and ugly of who they are, then I must apply this same compassion to myself in my own life. And you can do the same.

> " You can hold complex feelings about your elders while increasingly seeing them as people who are on their own journeys to find belonging.

=

"Hi, my Putri," she says softly.

I let out a sigh of relief. She still recognizes me.

Warmth starts to take over the anxiety that was pulsing through me when I first walked into Mama's nursing home room. My Dad is there, sitting in the floral armchair next to her bed, as he often does during visits. After forty-nine years of marriage, he's still by her side. He gets up, puts one arm around my shoulders, and pulls me close into the side of his body—a classic Punjabi dad embrace. I turn and put my arms around him, ensuring there's still a bit of space between my chest and his, and give him a squeeze. We've been doing a lot of hugging lately. Our souls need it in this gut-wrenching moment.

Mama is resting peacefully in her bed, which is where she now spends most of her time given that she can no longer walk. It's been a few days since I was last here, and since she's now in the palliative stage in her journey with Alzheimer's, I don't know what to expect when I visit. She's not using my name anymore, but she does still call me her beloved daughter. I'm clinging to her saying "Putri" as a gauge for whether she still knows who I am. Very shortly, she'll barely speak, and the signal will shift to her smiling and her eyes lighting up when she sees me.

Several months ago, when she'd see me walk into the sitting area on the memory floor, she'd often belt out, "My Putri, the motivational speaker!" channeling every bit of the voice of a former schoolteacher and causing heads to turn. Her burst of enthusiasm would always make me laugh. I long for those moments now. But, with every dip in her health, I push myself to anchor to the shreds of positivity that remain as this vicious terminal disease takes over the woman I still see as my hero.

We keep being told it's amazing she still remembers who we are and is in such good spirits in this late stage. I'm not surprised. In my heart, I know Mama Bhasin is a fighter. After all, I come from a long line of warrior princesses.

As I sit on her bed, I caress her face. She smiles at me. My heart fills with the knowing that the moment is coming up when I won't be able to do this anymore. Close to tears, I immediately distract myself by launching into talking to her about all the yummy treats I've brought for my Dad and her to enjoy. I don't know how much of what I'm sharing she understands, but I do know from past visits that if I cry, she will too. And it breaks my heart to see her weep without her being able to explain why.

With the front-row seat we have to watching my mother change at the hands of this illness, I'm struck by how her essence is still omnipresent. Over the years, as she's lost more and more of her memory, her spirit remains. As she's become quieter and quieter, I keep feeling her energy. Even as she becomes so weak she can barely move, it's still her.

As this all unfolds, I try my best to find stillness inside me. But, like everything else that's been hard in my life, I struggle to make this happen. Only this struggle is the worst I've ever experienced. I now understand why people say watching your parent die is life-altering. I'm feeling it now, and the pain is like a constant slashing to my heart that won't stop bleeding. The little girl in me still worships her mother and, in many respects, more than ever before.

Given how precious every minute has become, I focus on being as present as possible when I'm with her, reminding myself that this is the best and only moment I have. It's a powerful experience: caring for her has become the ultimate lesson on how to be more present.

I also commit to constantly telling her all the things I know one day down the road I'll be grateful I shared with her. It doesn't matter to me that she may not remember or understand most of it. What I care about is that I'm continuing to share what's in my heart with my Mom, the person who gave me life.

I especially never tire of telling her just how much I love her. Ever. I lose count of how many times I say these three words to her. Including today.

"I love you, my Mama," I say as I lay my head on her chest.

"I love you, my Putri," she replies as she lifts her frail hand to stroke my hair.

I'm not just Ritu Bhenji, I'm Ritu Putri. And my story began long ago.

TAKE A MOMENT TO REFLECT

What impact have your elders' stories had on your path to belonging?
Which of your elders have most influenced your experiences?

If your ancestral story was also marked by oppression, how did this affect your
elders' journeys to belong? How about your journey?

Have you talked with your elders about their childhood experiences growing
up? What insights do you hold from your conversations with them?

How did your elders' joy sway the energy and the flow of your upbringing?
How about their pain?

What mix of emotions comes up for you when you think about your elders?
How does reflecting on their belonging stories affect your
understanding of your emotions?

Questions for You to Explore Across All Chapters:

What are the key insights you've picked up from reading this chapter?

Which stories or messages most resonated with you? Why?

What are one or two things you'll do differently going forward?

CHAPTER THREE

BECOMING UGLY

I look up and he's staring directly at me. And very intently.

Heart pounding, I immediately look away.

"Why is the cutest guy in class watching me?" I wonder. I've been at the school for only a few months now, but I already know all the girls have a crush on him. And now, so do I.

Lucky for me, my desk faces his, so I get to steal peeks at him all day long. Since I'm only eleven years old, I have no idea how important this skill will become in my life's journey of checking out hot men.

I'm captivated by him. His blond hair is almost white, he has big, bright blue eyes that pop against his pinkish-white skin, he towers over the rest of the sixth graders, and when he's nervous he turns the same color as the hearts I secretly draw with a red marker around our initials in my notebook.

I look up in his direction. He's still staring. Our eyes lock.

A bunch of thoughts rush through my mind: Why won't he look away? What is he thinking? Does he like me too? Is everyone else noticing?

He opens his mouth to speak. I take a quick breath in anticipation.

"You have a beard, you know," he says very calmly. "You're so ugly."

I freeze. It's a sensation I will come to know well.

=

We come into the world deeply needing to be loved and to belong. As humans, we're animals, and as animals, we're one of the most social species out there. We're wired to deeply crave belonging in circles that love and accept us. We must have meaningful relationships to feel safe, healthy, and whole. And this is exactly why we're hungry for caring touches, supportive glances, warm smiles, soothing sounds, positive energy, words of affirmation, and anything that signals to us that we belong.

As babies, our bodies know this. And so, we literally cry out for belonging. In fact, when we're young, it's essential we feel acceptance so that we can unleash our glory. It's like we're clay waiting to have our magnificence unlocked by how we're molded. We're ready to be beautiful, strong, powerful, and wondrous—our potential is unlimited. How this is revealed depends on a bunch of things: the quality of the love and attention we get, if we're adored for who we are, how we're taken care of, what we're exposed to, who says what to us, and so much more.

> This chapter explores what happens to your sense of belonging when you constantly have hurtful experiences come your way as a child.

HATE, SHAME, AND BROKEN HEARTS

I came into the world believing in my ability to trust and be myself. I felt strong, confident, resilient, and ready to take things on. I know this because Mama Bhasin would repeatedly share the story of how my first words as a baby after "Mama" and "Dadda" were "Aapay! Aapay!" which means "I'll do it myself! I'll do it myself!" in Punjabi. Not "milk" or "bye" or "no" or "binky." My first words were a thundering affirmation of my autonomy, self-assurance, and determination.

I ponder this all the time—how I entered life with a bold warrior spirit. I had the will to do things on my own first, I believed in who I was, I felt good about myself, I wanted to achieve, and I wasn't afraid to declare my self-love. As a baby, my spirit knew of its greatness—just as yours did when you were born.

But along the way, so many of us come to believe we're ugly.

Over time, our self-beliefs are smothered by insecurities, self-doubts, limiting thoughts, negative narratives, and ultimately self-hate. Across our experiences, we internalize that something is wrong with us—that we're not good enough, that we're less worthy and deserving of love and acceptance, that we should suppress our authenticity by changing who we are, that we should hide our flaws because they affirm we're imperfect, that we ought to show up as curated personas so others can tolerate us, that we must defer to others' expectations rather that fulfill our own heart's desires, that we should self-loathe, and that we don't belong.

In essence, we lose connection with our greatness. Instead we fill with shame, which, as Brené Brown defines in her book *The Gifts of Imperfection*, is the intensely painful feeling of believing we're flawed and therefore unworthy of love and belonging. This is what our Performing Self mask and positivity-perfection-achievement armor help us to hide.

> We come into the world deeply needing to be loved and to belong. As humans, we're animals, and as animals, we're one of the most social species out there. We're wired to deeply crave belonging in circles that love and accept us.

Social rejection, alienation, insults, and abuse at anyone's hands can hurt us profoundly, and the lifelong effects can show up in several ways. They affect the extent to which we cultivate self-love; our comfort in speaking our truth; how we build bonds with others; how we show up at work; how much money we're able to earn; our levels of stress and tension in life; our craving to be our best; whether we find belonging; and so much more.

Not to mention that all of this can literally cause us to feel pain in our bodies, which is why constantly being on the receiving end of conditional love, put-downs, social isolation, and control over how we behave, especially as children, can be so harmful to our development and well-being.

So many of us grew up with hateful experiences that wounded us. For me, bullying broke my heart as a child.

≡

The principal is standing right behind me as we wait for the classroom door to open. I'm about to be introduced to my new sixth-grade classmates. It's partway through the school year, but it doesn't matter to me. While I'm a bit nervous, I'm mostly just excited to be in this new world where everything feels shiny and unique.

It's a massive financial stretch for my parents to move us away from our diverse working-class city neighborhood to this very White, affluent suburb. They could've shifted us to where so many of our Brown relatives and friends live, but they deliberately chose this supposedly idyllic area. They want us to get a better education, to access social networks they're not able to as new immigrants, and, as Brown kids growing up in White Canadian culture, to learn how to shift codes. It's not that they hate Punjabi culture and being Brown. Instead, both consciously and unconsciously, they're trying to protect us. They want to shield us from what they're experiencing.

But it doesn't work. While this decision will help me climb up the social ladder by several notches, it's also about to wreak havoc on the rest of my life.

As the door starts to open, the principal chirps, "Here we go, Ree-too! Your new class!" I walk into the room and hover at the front waiting for instructions on what to do next.

As I stand there, all sets of eyes are now on me, with pin-drop silence in the room. It's incredibly clear how stunned they are to see me.

Apparently, before we arrived, when my teacher revealed that a new student would be joining the class, it caused quite a stir. The boys started yelling, "Boy! Boy! Boy!" as they pounded their fists on the desks. Of course, the girls responded in kind. But they weren't expecting me. In a sea of whiteness, my brownness glaringly sticks out. I'm sporting a long braid that reaches well past my waist, with a part smack-dab through the center of my head. I'm stick-thin, and I'm rocking bushy eyebrows, arms, legs, and evidently cheeks. Plus, I have a bit of an overbite. (Very shortly, I'll come to add thick glasses and acne to this mix. They'll be wonderful additions.)

I'm wearing my red corduroy pants and my favorite pastel-pink sweater that has a bit of sheen in the knit. I enthusiastically picked out this outfit for this important moment. But, later in the day, I'll learn I'm "clashing," a concept I've never heard of before. I vow to never do that again.

My classmates' shock continues as the weeks and months and grades go by, and reminding me at every turn that I'm ugly is just the tip of the iceberg. The relentless bullying becomes a collective, orchestrated effort. There's the "I Hate Ritu" club, where you're either a member, which means both ignoring and taunting me, or you get bullied too. There are all kinds of drawings, including "Ritu, the Curry Queen," in addition to constant questions about why my clothes/shoes/house/car aren't nicer. And then there are the nonstop insults, teasing, and harassment about me, my "towel-rag-wearing" father, and my "freakish" family.

But it's not just that I look different and that I sometimes give off the scent of tarka (a combo of garlic, ginger, onion, tomato, and spices—or, put another way, like a heaping bowl of goat curry). It's that I'm bright, fiery, and peppy, and I'm unafraid to showcase my sass, especially when my parents aren't around. While I've already absorbed a stack of gendered messages around how I *ought* to behave, I still defy a lot of them. I'm unabashedly trying to do "me" as much as I can, which constantly rattles my parents. I struggle with the repercussions, but up until now, this hasn't been a problem at school.

My spirit is unfathomable to many of my new classmates, the cruel ones in particular—let's call them "The Mean Crew." They can't understand how someone who looks (and smells) like I do is so self-assured. They won't have it—they won't accept it—and so instead they work hard to drag me down. And they do.

As I stand by myself, recess after recess, hiding behind the portable classrooms to protect myself from harm, I pray to the Almighty Waheguru to make it stop. But it continues for years, well into high school. It becomes my own private hell, since I don't share what's happening with anyone, including at home with my parents where I've got a wholly different battle going on.

Over the decades of healing work it'll take to help address my wounds, I'll pick up a life-changing takeaway on belonging: we hate on others because we don't love ourselves, and we don't love ourselves because others hate on us.

In thinking back on my childhood experiences, I'll often reflect on who taught the kids at school to self-loathe so badly. I'll eventually come to a place where, while I still hurt at times, I'll finally feel beautiful inside and out. I'll wonder if they do too.

THE SLASHES FROM BEING BULLIED

When we stick out for whatever reason, we're walking targets for being bullied. And regardless of why it happens, bullies mercilessly rip at our souls by vilifying aspects of who we are that they know will hurt us, and constantly feeding us messages that we're unlovable, unworthy, and undeserving. Their words and actions cut us deeply, causing wounds that can take a lifetime to heal. This is especially true when we're the "lonely-only." By this I mean we're one of the sole people from a group that constantly experiences othering. So many of us were ridiculed, harassed, and assaulted because we were one of a few lonely-only kids in our neighborhoods and schools. And we did what we needed to do to cope, survive, stay safe, and navigate the mockery and humiliation, all while desperately craving belonging.

I think back to how I constantly felt lonely, insecure, and at risk of harm and abuse. I rarely felt like I belonged. I was a sitting duck just bracing myself, waiting for the next moment I'd be singled out, laughed at, and made fun of. The torment was all emotional, mental, and spiritual, and though I wasn't being hurt physically, the cruelty of being targeted and feeling rejected was more than enough to crush me.

I can recall all kinds of nasty moments growing up, like when I'd bring daal and rice to school for lunch, which resulted in wicked amounts of mockery. And even when I brought other things to eat, like Papa Bhasin's made-with-love and inspired-by-his-Italian-colleagues mortadella sandwiches, there'd be something else to call out. Like the time in high school when I was having lunch in the cafeteria and happened to be sitting at a table with a few of The Mean Crew. I noticed a hair poking out from my meat sandwich and, thinking it would only be a tiny piece, I subtly tried to remove it, only to horrify them all when I kept pulling... and pulling... and pulling... to set a foot-long strand of hair free. Once it was out, I wanted to keep eating, since everyone who lives in a long-haired Sikh household probably ingests about a pound of hair every year and usually doesn't bat an eye about it, but as if that would've gone down well! Its mere sight had already let loose enough anguish upon me.

Or I have recollections of pronouncing English words in class the way my parents did, only to have the whole room break out in laughter—teacher included—for not saying them the way the King of England would (if we ever meet in person, get me to tell you how I thought the word "appreciate" is pronounced). Or, given how reserved South Asian culture is around showing skin, I was petrified of taking my clothes off in the locker room in front of the other girls when we'd change for gym—a class I hated because I'd be picked last every time and then I'd have balls deliberately lobbed at my uncoordinated soul. So I basically learned to become a clothing contortionist, which of course I was harassed for. And I won't even get into the depth of the aversion I developed for my name given how often I was reminded of its proximity to the *Star Wars* robot R2-D2.

As hard as it is to think about painful experiences, this type of reflection is crucial in our journey to belong. In being tormented, we were being taught about the importance of maintaining society's existing hierarchies, along with messages about who is superior and therefore deserves to be at the top, and who is inferior and therefore should be at the bottom. And because of this, we were learning to speak less, to self-censor, to put down our hand, to lean out instead of leaning in, to let go of "Aapay! Aapay!" and to use our Performing Self mask and PPA armor to hide our essence. This helps us to better understand why we came up with a bunch of strategies to cope and survive. Like making ourselves invisible as much as possible. Or pushing down our differences and playing up our sameness. Or gluing on our mask and armor. Or standing quietly aside while others were being targeted. Or even bullying others ourselves.

> " We hate on others because we don't love ourselves,
> and we don't love ourselves because others hate on us.

Only now, through years of doing healing work, can I courageously admit I did all I just said to protect myself. And I can tell you: changing or hiding who you are will never lead to belonging.

When I mull over all the ways I performed in high school to "fit in," it makes me sigh. In being young and so wounded, I didn't understand the depth and impact of all that was happening to me like I do now. I'm thinking about how, around the age of fifteen, I convinced my parents to let me cut my long hair to shoulder length, which is significant as a Sikh. In Sikhi, we don't cut our hair for a few reasons, including that our unshorn hair is part of our unique identity and helps to signal that we're Sikhs, whether it's covered by a turban or a scarf, it's worn in a braid or a bun, or it's let loose and free. After fighting my parents for years to let me do this, I cut my beautiful lion's mane not because I was rejecting Sikhism but to shield myself from the bullying and in hopes that it would unlock the chance of belonging.

Once my hair was cut, I dyed it a frightening orange-ish for years. Even worse, at times I alternated between wearing green and blue contact lenses, which, with the orange-ish hair, was quite the sight to behold. And given my job at the local public library (epically nerdy and very on brand), I had voluminous access to baby books, and I almost changed Ritu to a "White name" (you would have known me as Carise Bhasin). The list goes on and on, but I'll stop here because I'm sure you're picking up on the funky picture I'm painting for you.

I started to deeply internalize that I needed to curb or mask my brownness for social doors to open, something I carried with me well into adulthood and that became a coping mechanism that took me years to unwire. But, in doing so, it also led me to feel like an outsider among my Brown family friends who were growing up in super-Brown neighborhoods. Yes, I was Punjabi just like them, but according to the cool kids in our family-friends' social circle, I was a "White-washed Oreo" on top of being "nerdy." Not to mention, I was dark-skinned for a Punjabi girl, so I didn't meet the bar for being viewed as pretty, which, as we know, is often required to make friends. So even within my own community, I felt like I didn't belong.

> There's so much power in owning and sharing our shame. When we unburden ourselves of the heaviness it brings, we come to see that our feelings of unworthiness are based on others' hate and not the truth of who we are.

And here's something else that's really heavy: one of the most painful outcomes of the bullying was that it pushed me to resent my parents—to be filled with shame about who they were, where they came from, and how I was born of them. And to add fuel to the fire, my negative feelings toward them were amplified by some of the adverse ways in which I was being parented. Or let me put this bluntly: they weren't helping the cause. I came to be in a place where I didn't want to be around them, seen with them, or connected with them. Rather than appreciate the magnitude of what they'd overcome and achieved, as I now do in every cell of my being, I was embarrassed and angry that my parents were Brown, long-haired, thick-accented immigrants.

It hurts to write this all out. But it's the truth of how I felt, so I must honor it—which reminds me of an important takeaway for our beautiful and hard journey to belong: we must reflect on what we went through growing up that led us to fill with shame about who we are, so we understand the healing work we need to do going forward.

There's so much power in owning and sharing our shame. When we unburden ourselves of the heaviness it brings, we come to see that our feelings of unworthiness are based on others' hate and not the truth of who we are. Even though I constantly felt low and I struggled with the darkness that came with "becoming ugly," I knew I was experiencing injustice. I knew that I deserved more. I can even remember saying to myself around the age of twelve or thirteen, "One day I'll be a household name and they'll know how to say my name right." I wanted to come alive. I just didn't know how to tap into my spark.

≡

I have him pinned up against the lockers, his jacket balled up in each of my fists. Just inches away from my face, I can see his hazel eyes watering and red, splotchy patches forming on his lily-white cheeks.

Just days earlier, while on a bathroom break from my math class, I run into my sister, Komal, crying in the hallway outside of her ninth-grade geography class. The substitute teacher is consoling her. I hear for the first time that a few boys have been picking on her lately, but today has been particularly bad. Apparently, our "Paki" mom spreads like peanut butter.

"It can happen to me, but I won't let it happen to them," I often say to myself when I look at my younger siblings. I can feel ugly because of hate, but I don't want them to. I'm Ritu Bhenji, and, even though I'm struggling to do this for myself, it's my duty to protect them. It's this same belief that leads me to ride my bike to the street corner where my brother catches his school bus to threaten the lives of the kids who have been taunting him. My siblings' encounters with bullies are sporadic, and I want to help keep it that way. I can harass them because I'm their older sister and, in being bullied myself, I've learned how to do this—but no one else is allowed to.

As I watch Komal weep in the high school hallway, I feel rage rip through me. Marching into the now unsupervised classroom, I demand the kids tell me who the culprits are. One is named—that's all I need.

I now have him against the lockers, literally in my hands. It's just me, him, and some of his friends who are staring at me like a herd of deer in headlights. They dare not move.

"If you ever say anything to my sister again, you'll deal with me," I scream into his face. He manages to muster a nod as tears roll down his face. As I let him go, his feet drop to the ground.

I whip around, but quickly turn back to give him the look of death—the same look I've been getting for years. They've trained me well.

And then I stomp off.

He never bothers her again.

My private hell continues.

But now, the "I will no longer be a doormat" whispers have started. And I realize if I can do this for them, then I must learn to do this for me.

TAKE A MOMENT TO REFLECT

How would you describe your childhood? What highlights do you recall from back then? What tough moments do you remember?

Were you bullied as a child? If so, how did bullying affect you? How does the effect still show up for you now as an adult, if at all?

What other childhood experiences impacted your journey to belong? Did you learn to "become ugly" too? How did this happen for you? How do you feel this inside you now?

What coping strategies did you use to protect yourself growing up? How did this help you? How does this hurt you now?

Questions for You to Explore Across All Chapters:

What are the key insights you've picked up from reading this chapter?

Which stories or messages most resonated with you? Why?

What are one or two things you'll do differently going forward?

CHAPTER FOUR

LEARNING THAT LIFE IS A STAGE

Standing behind the side curtains, I sense the buzz filling the auditorium. It's both exhilarating and nauseating. I can feel my stomach churning and I want to run screaming from the building, though I know that's not an option. This is a big moment for me. In fact, it's a first—I've never given a speech on a stage before. It's too early to know that down the road I'll do this thousands of times.

I poke my head out to peer at the crowd. A few hundred students are sitting cross-legged on the floor, squirming as they listen to the kid who's speaking right now. The churning gets stronger, as does the desire to escape. But again, I'm not going anywhere.

I "made it to the gym." It's huge to be selected to represent your class at the school speech competition. What I can't get over is that The Mean Crew chose me. I guess they had no choice since my speech about the joy of living life as a pair of sneakers destroyed everyone else's. They want to win the school trophy and place it on the ledge at the front of our classroom. Though they hate me, I'm their best shot. The irony of this moment is not lost on me, even at the age of eleven. But it doesn't matter. I'll take any crumbs that come my way.

I'm feeling an unparalleled level of anxiety, made bigger by my father being in the audience. Given how special this experience is, my Dad has taken time off from his quality-control job to come watch me present. Wearing his bright maroon turban. In the gym. Where everyone can see him. I both am embarrassed and want to protect him. The nausea is overwhelming, and I'd throw up, except that I already did an hour ago. As a treat, he took me for lunch at McDonald's, but everything I ate came barreling out the second I got back to school. Of course, I don't tell him this. I don't want to worry him. He's already got so much on his plate. I'm also Bhenji to my parents.

"Ree-too, it's time," the teacher who's overseeing this affair calls out to me. "Go on now. You'll be great!"

This is it. The moment I've been waiting for, where I'll finally be seen and heard. But I'm terrified. And what's making it worse is that I can't bring myself to name how scared I am—not to this teacher, not to my own teacher, not to my classmates, not to my Dad, not to anyone. I need to be "strong" as much as possible. I'm being taught that this is a good thing. The problem is that there's a line between being a warrior and a gladiator, and being pushed to be the latter at such a young age will hurt me down the road.

It may be the first time I'm on a stage giving a speech, but I've already learned how important it is to perform—to curate and hide aspects of who I am and how I feel, think, and behave. In so many ways, my life will become a giant play, one where the main actor puts on the performance of a lifetime. It'll strike at my ability to experience belonging, but this is a truth that'll take me time to learn.

"Ree-too, is everything okay?" the teacher softly asks.

"Yes! I'm ready!" I brightly exclaim, putting on the big smile that'll become tantamount to my Performing Self mask and positivity-perfection-achievement armor.

I take a big breath and start to walk out. Silence fills the room. When I hit the center of the stage, I realize it's too late to run. I pause to scan the crowd, hoping it'll make me feel better. But it has the opposite effect. All I can see is an ocean of whiteness. And my Dad's maroon turban. Which reminds me that he took a day off from work to be here. But that's enough to activate the Bhenji in me. I open my mouth and the words start to pour out.

Of course, I kick ass because I've already internalized that failing is not an option. But I'm disqualified. I brought a pair of sneakers onto the stage as a prop.

The teachers knew I was going to do this, but none of them stopped to tell me this was against the rules. Had I known, I wouldn't have done it. It becomes an early life lesson about who gets to access the rules and who doesn't. I'll see this unfairness replicated again and again in the years to come. It'll be one of the reasons why I'll eventually launch my global inclusion firm.

But right now, I'm crestfallen. And so is my class. The Mean Crew ignore me for being the loser they think I am. I berate myself for the imperfection of not winning—while I feel the injustice pulse through me for being eliminated for something I didn't know I wasn't allowed to do. And because I've already learned that life is a stage where I must mask and armor up, I don't share my rage with anyone. Not a soul. Like I do with almost everything that happens to me as a kid, I eat my pain. Yes, the day will come when I'll effortlessly raise hell when I experience inequities—and I'll feel solid as a rock while doing it. But I'm nowhere near that place right now. Suppressing my hurt is how I'm learning to navigate the world.

So life carries on with my mask, my armor, my stage, and my hurt.

$$\equiv$$

Many of us learn about the importance of creating a Performing Self as children—a self that changes, masks, and pushes down who we are and how we want to behave. It's like a constructed persona we put out there because we feel we *have to* and not because we *want to*. What we want is to belong. We long to be accepted by the people around us. But the problem is that they judge us. So we change how we behave. Because if we don't, we worry they'll hate us. That they'll reject us. That they'll shame us. This fear is why our Performing Self feels like a useful shield to protect us from hurt.

And here's a heavy takeaway: many of us learned to perform well before the world began to pick on us. It started in our homes. Because we were bullied before we were bullied.

> This chapter reveals the importance of understanding the impact your upbringing can have on your sense of belonging.

BEING MOLDED INTO SOMEONE YOU'RE NOT

From the moment we were born, in how our elders molded and shaped us, they etched their rules on the "right way" to behave on our souls. While some of us were blessed with light touches and the freedom to just be, many of us were blasted with all kinds of "don't do thises" and "don't do thats" on how to behave. It started innocently enough, with warnings like "Don't touch that because you'll hurt yourself" or a big smile when we held a spoon properly. But then it turned into shaming like "Why are you laughing so loud?!" or a disgusted look when they checked out what we wanted to wear. And then it morphed into more direct commands like "You're never to bring home X-type-of-person" or the silent treatment for days when we shared that we didn't want to study Y to become Z. The labyrinth of messages that came our way led us to believe that we're broken and in need of fixing. And it really hurt.

That said, I'm confident our elders didn't sit down at a table together and say, "Let's really try to mess up our children by killing their spirit." I know now they were doing their best based on what they knew. But in the complicated ways in which many of us were raised, we got all kinds of mixed messaging around the "right way" to behave, which taught us to self-loathe.

When I think back to my childhood, I realize my parents weren't deliberately trying to hurt me by giving me clashing and confusing rules around how to straddle both Punjabi and White Canadian cultures. But that's what happened, and it was so tricky to navigate.

On one end, we did a lot of "White things" that weren't common for Brown immigrant folks to do back then: I took swimming and ballet lessons; I did summer art classes where I learned to paint with watercolor; we went to cottages and swam in freezing-cold lakes where Mama Bhasin rocked a bikini and Papa Bhasin wore tight trunks; we went camping in the woods and slept in tents; and my parents hung out with a lot of White people and encouraged me to do the same. So I said, "Okay, I'll throw myself into White Canadian culture," which also aligned with the "be like us" messages I was bombarded with at school. For me, part of this meant feeling free to assert myself. And sometimes my parents were fine with this spirit, like when I decided to launch into child entrepreneurship by becoming the neighborhood magician (not joking). Or when I told them I wanted to live in a Costa Rican rainforest for a semester of high school as part of an international development course, with two White Canadian girls and three random Costa Rican ranger men, and they agreed (really not joking).

But then there were all the "oh hell no" moments, signaling that I'd gone too far. I can still hear them telling me off in Punjabi in my head, which is so much spicier than English. There was the how-dare-you-become-mouthy/sassy/liberated-like-your-White-friends messaging: "You think we're White?! Don't talk to me like a White kid!" And then there was the this-isn't-a-democracy-where-you-have-freedom commentary: "What?! You want to sleep over at insert-White-girl's-name's house?! You go, we all go!" and "No, you are never allowed to talk to boys, ever. Not until you're married."

Basically, while my parents were fine with me absorbing some aspects of White Canadian culture, they mostly wanted me to be Indian. And by this I'm talking about taking on the stereotype of the "perfect high-society Indian child": being a combo of brilliant and nerdy, obedient and deferential, very attractive but chaste, seen but not heard, talented but passive, and successful but humble. It meant talking, laughing, gesturing, dressing, and emoting in a very specific way. It also meant acting like everything was perfectly wonderful when we were in public, even when the opposite was true. To do otherwise would violate the "Life can only be beautiful" commandment and, may the gods help us all, "What will society think?!" If I had a 22-karat gold coin straight from Mother India for every time I heard that question growing up, I'd be retired and living on a white sandy beach right now.

But, of course, my naturally feisty, energetic, animated, and high-volume ways didn't mesh with the desired archetype. I was like a bull in an Indian bone china shop. So this is how my Performing Self mask, my positivity-perfection-achievement armor, and I became besties. As I continued to push down my essence, I played up my PPA to help shield me from critique. And because it usually worked, I became good at doing it.

For all of us who did this growing up, just because it worked doesn't mean it was good for us, nor does it mean we were experiencing actual belonging. The problem is that when we performed and projected PPA, we were rewarded with warmth and praise, kind of like winning a prize. But when we didn't—when we showed up authentically—it often felt like love was being taken away and, even worse, we were being punished.

In receiving conditional love, it's not surprising our feelings of worthiness and belonging started to hinge on whether we followed the rules. Which is why in high school, I started to fight back against my parents' rules. I was desperate to claim more freedom—and, as Ritu Bhenji, I was doing it for both me and my siblings. I just didn't get why my parents wouldn't ease up: I was a straight A student (except for gym); I won awards; I volunteered; I had a range of part-time jobs and side hustles (recall: magician); and I (mostly) wasn't drinking, smoking, having sex, or doing other things that Indian society deemed as "bad behavior."

I was just being a teenager, trying to find her way—only I felt upset *and* guilty about doing this, which led to some troubling moments between my parents and me. Early on in high school, I ended up being kicked out of the house for a few weeks, which was unheard of in South Asian culture back then and even now. I stayed with a White friend's family because, let's be real, other Indian parents wouldn't have taken me in. It would've been seen as an epic betrayal, and they would've dragged me by my braid back home ASAP. Ultimately, the school's guidance counselor helped us to reconcile, and my parents enlisted the support of a family therapist to get us through this moment. But my pain continued. I felt so lost and disconnected from everyone around me—it was like I didn't "fit in" anywhere.

In my loneliness and despair, I even went through a period where I felt suicidal, like there was no other way I would be able to escape the pain I felt. This is something I've never talked candidly about before, including with my parents. In the early nineties, there were no resources to support the mix of cultural, mental health, and racist-bullying issues I was having, but I'm blessed to have had the same guidance counselor and a few friends help get me through this dark time. And, if you've ever wondered if counseling hotlines are used and if they help, I'm living proof that they are and that they do. I can remember repeatedly calling Kids Help Phone, a Canadian nonprofit organization that offered telephone counseling (they now do online too) to youth in need—and I'm so grateful I did.

When I think back to these moments now, it makes my heart hurt. But I know for my healing work it's important that I reflect on my childhood journey—as it is for you to do with yours.

At the end of the day, my parents could tell I was suffering and that they had something to do with it. They may not have known why and how deeply, but they loved me and wanted me to be happier, so they finally opened up to some change. Hang on to your hats/turbans/wraps/head scarves, everyone! Later on in high school, I earned the freedom to stay out at night until 1 a.m.; go to dances, parties, and clubs; go away for university (as in, live in residence and not at home); and, most wildly, openly date boys, including, at the age of seventeen, inviting over my first real boyfriend, a nice White guy, who became a fixture in our household.

While I know how difficult these experiences were for me as a child of immigrants, I now have a better sense of how tough this must have been for our immigrant elders. By pushing us to perform, it's not that they were deliberately trying to sabotage our joy or ruin our lives. They were grappling with how to find belonging in new countries; many of them were replicating the parenting tools their elders had used to bring them up; and they were working hard to raise children, mostly without piles of resources, support, and role models. Plus, they were also trying to shield us from the hate and hardships they were experiencing by teaching us behaviors they believed would help us to live better. They didn't realize they were passing their hurt along to us.

> 66 We can love and honor our elders for the wonderful ways in which they've influenced our lives, while being honest about the harmful impact of some aspects of their parenting.

This realization takes me back to the complicated mashup of emotions so many of us are filled with when we think about our upbringings. While we're flooded with love and gratitude when we reflect on how our elders raised us, we're also overcome by a mix of guilt, bitterness, fury, pain, and regret when we think about how they've pressured us to perform. It's a reminder of how hard life and the path to belonging can be. This offers a powerful takeaway: we can love and honor our elders for the wonderful ways in which they've influenced our lives, while being honest about the harmful impact of some aspects of their parenting.

That's what makes our lives beautiful. And makes us real.

As much as I know that I'm wounded from parts of my upbringing, I love my parents dearly. I'm so grateful to be the daughter of Mama Bhasin, a brilliant, sassy, feisty, witty, and fun woman. I'm so proud to be the daughter of Papa Bhasin, an unbelievably hard-working, resilient, sharp, kind, and thoughtful man. I truly believe to my core that had it not been for their sacrifices, love, and support, I wouldn't be where I am in my life and the person I am today. So I'm throwing them and all the elders who touched my life some love, and I hope you're up for doing the same.

≡

I plunk myself on a seat at the front of the room because I know it'll force me to pay attention during the workshop. Earlier this afternoon I delivered a keynote at the conference I'm at, and I've convinced myself to attend this breakout session on anti-oppression. The competing option was to hunt down the nearest Saks OFF 5TH to check out the fashion deals (hail to my immigrant household upbringing), but I knew this would be better for my brain and soul. And I was right. I quickly get sucked into what's being taught, time is flying by, and we're now onto an exercise. We're told to find a partner and then talk about oppressive messages from our childhoods that impact us as adults. I turn to the person sitting to my right. We smile at each other warmly.

After I introduce myself and talk a bit about my cultural background, I learn my partner is a Black American woman, also cis and hetero, in her fifties. As it happens, she's a lawyer, too, but unlike me, who gave up the practice of law after about five seconds, she's now a partner at a prestigious law firm, which isn't an easy feat for a White man, let alone a Black woman, given how entrenched misogynoir is in the corporate world.

There's something about our connection that moves me to immediately start pouring out my heart. I start by describing the trauma-inducing world my elders experienced given India's colonization, and then talk about my parents' difficult journey to find belonging in Canada. I say to her, "You know, being othered just felt very normal to me, since I saw it nonstop with my parents. But it also happened to me from a young age, so I just accepted it as a way of life."

I go on to confide that I still bear the wounds from how I was treated by The Mean Crew, not to mention the strict and confusing parenting I received, and that I still feel so messed up and struggle to belong at times. I name that I know exactly why I became fixated with my Performing Self mask and PPA armor, which kept me on a stage putting out a curated act around my identities, until I went to the ashram. I even let out how I'm still filled with shame about aspects of who I am, including sitting here with her in this very moment, as a single woman in her late thirties.

As I speak, I can tell she's absorbing my words and spirit, because of how intently she's listening and how warm her energy feels.

> " When it comes to experiencing hardships, while we may be slashed by different knives, we're drawn to caring for each other because we know how much a cut can hurt.

She opens up about how she grew up poor and was raised primarily by her grandparents, descendants of people who were enslaved in the U.S. for generations. She became a lawyer, but at every turn, she experienced all kinds of barriers connected to her identities. From classroom to boardroom, she's constantly the lonely-only Black woman at the table; she has her own version of a mask, armor, and stage; and she too struggles to find belonging. But then, here she is, smashing ceilings.

She also vulnerably reveals that in wanting to protect her from society's harm, her grandparents taught her to *not* make eye contact with "important people," especially when they're White. They told her to "avert her eyes"—as in, look down or look away.

"In learning to avert my eyes, I learned to avert my spirit."

Chilling. She then goes on to say that she still averts her spirit by not being her authentic self because, deep in her heart, she continues to carry feelings of shame and unworthiness.

Her words are unforgettable because I understand exactly what she means. Through the hurtful, hateful, and harmful things that've come my way, I've also learned to avert my spirit. To smother my spark. And I know how hard it is to break free. We both cry as we share our stories, and we weep as we listen. Sadly, we don't exchange our personal information, and years later, when I think about her, I won't be able to recall her name or where she works. But, and as another life takeaway, I continue to send her love and blessings through the energetic waves in the Universe, knowing she'll receive the goodness I'm directing her way—something you can always do when someone has touched your life.

As I leave the conference center, I'm reminded of how hard it can be to interrupt the pull toward living life as though we're performing on a stage. And I'm starting to deeply understand that it isn't just me who's struggling with this— this is a collective experience, especially for those of us who constantly have hate coming our way. It's also a moment that highlights how, when it comes to experiencing hardships, while we may be slashed by different knives, we're drawn to caring for each other because we know how much a cut can hurt.

TAKE A MOMENT TO REFLECT

As you read my childhood stories, what memories from your own upbringing came up for you?

What rules around how to behave did you get from your elders while growing up? How did you feel about this at the time? How do you feel now? What has been the impact on how you behave?

To what extent did you feel the need to perform—either change or hide who you are—while growing up to feel accepted? What did performing look like for you? How did it help you?

How did your elders teach you to avert your eyes, if at all? How does the tendency to avert your eyes show up for you now? How does it affect your sense of belonging?

Questions for You to Explore Across All Chapters:

What are the key insights you've picked up from reading this chapter?

Which stories or messages most resonated with you? Why?

What are one or two things you'll do differently going forward?

CHAPTER FIVE

OUR BODIES HURT

'm standing buck naked in front of the full-length mirror in my bedroom. The Indian girl in me feels awkward about having no clothes on, even when I'm by myself. But it's needed for the inspection that's going to take place before I head to brunch with some friends.

I'm about to start the "pinch test," which is what happens when I spend time tugging at folds of skin across my body to check for expansion. My inner saboteur, The Voice, the ruthless and highly vocal judge who lives in my head, will join me for the assessment. I'm a hundred and eighteen pounds soaking wet, and we're both determined to keep it this way. We'll be using a scoring card based on the rampant messaging out there about what's beautiful and what's not.

First, I pull at the right side of my waist. *Not bad*, says The Voice.

I then move down to my stomach to grab at the flesh there. The Voice sighs.

Slowly, I make my way to my inner thighs to take hold of the squishiness. *So gross,* sneers The Voice.

Next up is my butt. But I can't bring myself to turn around and look at its reflection while I squeeze it. I can't handle the sight of the dimples, cellulite, and stretch marks that cover my tush. And neither can The Voice. It feels like it's been months since I last found the courage to check out what it looks like without clothes on.

Feels flabby, The Voice says. Followed by *You're so flabby*.

I know, The Voice, I know.

For the last stop, I bring my face a few inches away from the mirror, taking turns slanting my head at various angles to catch the light. I'm studying my skin for pimples, lines, blemishes, hair, and anything else that'll make it less than perfect.

Well done! cheers The Voice.

I exhale. I got something right.

I'm in my late twenties, and I've been attacking my body this way for over fifteen years now. I'll keep doing this for at least another decade before I realize how badly this practice and others are harming me and my soul.

I slip on black underclothes that are matching because to not be coordinating would be pedestrian and violate my perma-perfection code. While no one else will see what's happening under my clothes, I'll know. And so, every layer must be in order. But as I reach for my mid-rise jeans, I catch a glimpse of the microscopic "muffin top" that's now formed over my underwear's waistband. I snarl in disgust and so does The Voice, who scolds me for not working out enough this past week, and then instructs me to only consume smoothies for the next few days. I agree.

I'm just grateful my belly isn't popping out today. We're merciless when I look five months pregnant even though I'm not. Sadly, we're too preoccupied with being the judgment police to notice my gut is desperately trying to send me a signal: it's bloated and sticking out because of the emotional pain I'm holding inside me, not because of how much I'm eating. I have no idea of this—yet.

With my jeans and crop-top now on, I do a 360 in the mirror. *See, you can be pretty,* declares The Voice.

I get what The Voice is saying. My parents' genes have kicked in: I'm tall and thin, which I'm hell bent on maintaining; I've filled out in coveted areas; the braces have helped to get me closer to my Dad's naturally flawless smile; and, although too dark by South Asian standards, my skin is smooth and even. And there's more still: thankfully laser hair removal machines were invented, and my fur is almost gone; my fixation on working out is keeping me tight and trim; and I've become a fancy lawyer type who now dresses to impress. I'm doing all the "right things."

I've come a long way from the time when the boys in The Mean Crew would tell me no guys will ever like me because of all the hot girls out there. I'm no longer the "ugly Paki who needs to shave her face." I'm finally coming up as one of the hot girls for some.

But angst, confusion, and shame continue to plague me.

Most Brown men and their daughter-in-law-hunting parents won't look in my direction because I'm "too dark," on top of being too feisty. But that doesn't matter to me because lots of White boys and guys from other cultures are all about me. I'm *exotic* and a *challenge*, they say. These words snap at me like a rubber band hitting my skin. But The Voice is there in the background directing me to pay no mind to the sting and instead to take these messages as a compliment. So, I do. I'm still grasping for any crumbs that come my way, so I'm okay with being the yo-yo that goes with this. I'm in a giant haze where I can't tell just how problematic this all is.

As I take one last look at myself in the mirror, my gaze moves to the few inches of my exposed tummy. It's edgy for me to sport this look. Papa Bhasin doesn't love when I dress like this because of what people will think about me. But he knows better than to say anything, for fear that I'll bite his turbaned head off. He's not wrong: I'm just a few years out of college, and my feminist flag is always at full staff. But I'm not thinking about my Dad and his "What will society think?!" mentality in this moment. My mind is racing with thoughts about my recent experience being stalked. When the police updated me after cautioning the man who had brought hell into my life, they told me to "be careful" going forward. I'm wondering if wardrobe decisions are part of what they meant.

I decide to leave my outfit as is and instead grab my jacket for any insecure moments. As I open the front door to head out, The Voice calls out, *Let's see what you'll have to deal with today.* This is in reference to how I'm going to handle any hurtful-hateful-harmful stuff that comes my way. But because I'm often numb, I'm ready.

"Don't you worry, The Voice. I'm on it. As always," I reply.

And with that, I straighten my back, yank at the bottom of my shirt, push my chest forward, tilt my chin up, and march out into the world.

=

Back when I was a kid in primary school, one of my teachers hung a poster on the wall showcasing the nursery rhyme "Sticks and stones may break my bones, but words will never hurt me." The bright-blue cursive writing was surrounded by a bunch of colorful flowers.

When I think of this now, I'm reminded of how, from the moment we're born, we start being conditioned to suppress the pain in our body that's caused by the harm coming our way. And it's a raging affirmation of how when we're growing up, along with performing, at every step along the way we're taught to disconnect from our body, including through pretty artwork. It's one of the reasons I ended up in front of the mirror in my late twenties attacking myself with the pinch test. And it explains why many of us can't feel that our body is literally hurting, which is blocking us from experiencing greater belonging.

> This chapter explores how you can end up both carrying hurt in your body and learning to hurt your body, impacting your ability to belong.

BEING MEAN TO YOUR BODY

Throughout our lives, we absorb messages about the importance of ignoring and overriding many of the emotions and sensations that come up in our body, especially when they're caused by shame. This happens so often and in such a forceful way, we don't always know it's happening.

But even sadder, because of how detached many of us have become from our bodies, we come to treat our castle like it's a hard shell we can hate on, kick around, and pick at. And we do this while playing around with decorating it based on all of society's messages about what our body is supposed to look like. We're mean to our body. We bully our body. In doing this, we move further and further away from the important truth that we *are* our body. When we neglect what we're feeling inside or we torment our body, we ultimately hurt our core self—our essence. And in doing so, we stop belonging to ourselves.

I started internalizing messages that my body was fair game for anyone's assessment from a very young age. My earliest memory of learning to hate on my body was around the age of five. I remember playing "teatime" with a few White girls from my neighborhood using my Royal Doulton-inspired white-and-blue-flowered plastic tea set. (So colonial when I think about it now!) There I was, filling each of our cups with "tea" out of the cute little teapot, when one of the girls asked me why one side of my hands was white and the other side was brown.

My innocent and honest reply was "I don't know." I didn't have the benefit of pulling out my phone and cobbling together the following oversimplified response: melanin is basically the pigment found in our skin, and other body parts, that gives us color. The more melanin we have, the darker our skin. And the palms of our hands have less melanin than most of the skin on our bodies.

What I do know is that they added mud into my cup and forced me to drink the dirty water. Just because my body wasn't like theirs. Their message was clear: You should feel ashamed about your skin, about your body, about who you are.

You are less worthy.

You don't belong.

In picking on my body, they were teaching me how to bully myself. And, as a fast learner, I absorbed this quickly. Every other signal that came my way after this point, whether directly or indirectly, helped to both affirm their message and gave me more ammunition for how I could attack myself. How I could keep averting my spirit. And, as a Punjabi, Sikh, Brown, Canadian woman straddling many worlds, there was so much ammo! From my body shape to my skin tone to my hair (both on my head and all over my body), the mixed messaging about how to treat my body was—and continues to be—overwhelming. The impact has been profound.

From Indian culture, I picked up that I should eat more rotis because I looked sickly thin and needed curves to look good in a sari, like the Bollywood babes in the movies we'd watch on Saturday afternoons. But then, on the other hand, in American-influenced Canadian culture, my slim figure was on point. And, in fact, it was one of the few areas about which no one could really say anything negative to me because I was the "ideal." So, of course, I was committed to staying this way.

When I was younger, I tried almost every diet fad out there, even though the last thing I needed to do was starve my body of nutrients. I prioritized working out over sleep and other forms of R&R, and over having a healthy state of mind. Since bigger butts weren't the rage back then, I was desperate to shrink the size of my tush to the point where, when I was a teenager, I permanently damaged the flooring in front of the family room TV. The carpet lifted and a creaky sound emerged in the spot where, several times a week, I'd do episodes of *20 Minute Workout* while taking instructions from the neon-pink legwarmer-wearing Farrah Fawcett lookalikes.

> " When we neglect what we're feeling inside or we torment our body, we ultimately hurt our core self—our essence. And in doing so, we stop belonging to ourselves.

Then there was the constant battle with how much of my body I should showcase for the world to see. In one corner of the ring was Indian culture telling me to cover up my goodies and be a clothing contortionist. This messaging was so prevalent, I even put a pair of my baby brother's shorts onto my childhood teddy bear to cover up his "shame-shame," which is what many of us, in Indian culture, were taught to call the areas of our body where the sun doesn't shine. In the other corner was American-influenced Canadian culture, shouting the puzzling mix of "Show it all! But wait, that's too much! No, no, give us more! Slow down now, you've gone too far. Men will come for you, and it will be *your* fault." It was enough to make my brain explode.

But there was one area where the messaging was consistent and there was no confusion: the fairer your skin tone, the better. From the White dolls I was gifted to the fashion magazines filled with White faces; from TV shows like *Beverly Hills, 90210* that reinforced the glamor of being White to hurtful taunts at school for being darker skinned; from the "exotic" comments from White men like "Ooh, I love your almond-shaped eyes. You look like Pocahontas" to the "don't sit in the sun" directives from my elders—it was omnipresent and rampant.

All that and more is what led me, when I was younger, to repeatedly have one-way conversations with the Highest asking to decrease my melanin so that I'd have lighter skin, auburn hair, hazel eyes, and rosy-pink areolae. I'd tried everything from covering my face with a thick, gritty mix of besan—a.k.a. chickpea flour—to "brighten and lighten" my skin to rocking, as I already shared, the hideous combo of green contact lenses with orange-bleached hair. For a while, I even tried slathering truckloads of cream on my darker-skinned knees to help them become lighter.

Given all the messages swirling around me about how I didn't belong, who could blame me for my efforts? Not to mention, there were dozens of moments when, at family parties and Punjabi wedding receptions, my elders would come up to me and my sister and say something to the effect of the following:

To Sister Bhasin, with her "fair" skin, lighter eyes and hair, almost 5'10" height, and hourglass figure: "There she is, the Indian beauty queen!"

Then, in the very next breath, to me, with my darker brown skin, eyes, and hair, almost 5'7" height, and emaciated (by their standards) physique: "Ritu! The lawyer!"

For the record, I'm not embellishing. And how about this: not once after these awful moments did Komal and I turn to each other and say, "Wow, that was really frogged up! How evil and wrong is that messaging?!" If it were to happen to us today, we'd set the person straight by using the strategies I'll explore in *Belonging*. But back then, both of us were too ashamed to even talk about it. I now know from sharing our own healing journeys that as I walked away feeling ugly, she'd walk away feeling stupid and objectified.

When and how our society agreed that everyone has the right to vocalize their opinions, especially hateful ones, about other people's bodies, I have no idea. But it must stop given how harmful this is to our sense of belonging.

OUR BODIES LITERALLY HURT

It's not just the way we look that attracts hurtful messaging. As I've been revealing, hate can come our way about absolutely anything and from absolutely anyone. Whether the judgment is about the size of our body, the darkness of our skin, who our parents are, how we speak, what faith we practice, who we want to love, how we want to spend our time, or what our flaws are—whatever it is, directly or indirectly, when people signal that we don't belong, we can hold the hurt inside us.

When I say inside us, yes, we hold the hurt in our minds—we can start to believe we're less intelligent, competent, lovable, worthy, and beautiful. And this can lead us to spend hours thinking about how people hate on us and then blasting ourselves for not doing anything to stop them. Or we self-flog about why we've let it upset us or why this always happens to us. Or we feel inferior and like impostors. Or we change and hide who we are. Or we tell ourselves horrible things like "See, this is why I'm such a loser."

But our mind isn't where we hold the lion's share of our pain; our body is. And this is why it's important that we pay attention to the hurt we're carrying inside us. When we experience hate, rejection, disapproval, judgment, or anything that feels like disrespect, the body can interpret this as a threat to its safety—it can feel like it's being attacked or about to be. And this in turn can lead our nervous system, which is like the main switchboard in our body, to become activated. Everyone's activation will look different, but you may notice your heart starts to pound, your breaths get shorter and faster, you're suddenly sweating, tension spreads throughout your insides, or you feel numb all over.

> **Our mind isn't where we hold the lion's share of our pain; our body is.**

When our nervous system is constantly being activated because of hurtful experiences, it can cause us to hold trauma in our body. The source of the activation and resulting trauma may be different for each of us, but the outcome is the same: it can lead to serious health issues if we don't work to heal it. Unhealed trauma can have a serious, adverse impact across the systems in our body, from our skin, digestion, blood pressure, and muscles to our anxiety, depression, memory, and so much more.

When I reflect on all the difficult experiences I've endured that have led to heightened activation in my body, it doesn't surprise me that I've struggled with tummy issues, restless sleep, inflamed skin, back and neck pain, and diminished mental health. My body literally hurts from all the harmful and hateful things that've come my way, which is another reason why I've come to rely so heavily on healing practices along my journey to belong.

To show you what it can look like to hold hurt in our body, I want to share a heartbreaking moment that still pains me, and I suspect it'll be hard for a lot of you to take in as well. It's about racialized hate and violence, so if you want to skip over this story and go right to the next chapter, please do. (Know that, in *Healing*, I'm going to talk all about how we can settle our body when we feel activated.)

=

It's August 5, 2012. I'm still in my pajamas, puttering around my condo as I often do midday on a lazy Sunday. Smoothie in hand, I plunk down onto the couch when a wave of nausea suddenly hits me. I was out late partying, and I groan as I realize I'm a bit hungover. It's going to be one of those days.

I start flicking through the channels looking for something light for my foggy brain. I quickly skip over all the prayer programming and the kids' shows and start looking for the cheesy movies. Even a Bollywood film would do right about now. As I click away on the remote control, I pass through a few news stations, including CNN, where an image catches my eye. I immediately go back.

I freeze at the sight of what's on the screen: there's been an attack on a Sikh gurdwara in Oak Creek, Wisconsin, where a white supremacist killed several worshippers and is now dead himself.

It's late morning in Wisconsin, so I can vividly picture what was likely happening in the gurdwara when the shooter decided to release evil. This is when many worshippers, and especially seniors and immigrants, come early to do seva, or volunteer their time, to prepare for the day's program. This includes cooking up the langar, the yummy veggie meal that's offered after service. It's before the sangat, the congregation, arrives for the services, so while it's not packed with people, there's still an energetic buzz filling the air.

The gurdwara vibrates with energy at this time of day. You can hear the voices of people chattering away as they make roti after roti in the kitchen. Little kids run up and down the halls laughing and playing while elders chase after them.

The sound of kirtan music flows out of the speakers in the hallways. And this is all happening against a backdrop of spiritual calmness that makes a gurdwara one of my favorite places in the world to be.

This is what I'm imagining as I stare at the screen, only I'm picturing it being destroyed by the sounds of gunfire and people screaming, the feelings of panic and chaos, and the sight of gore everywhere. I imagine the innocent souls covered in blood, dead on the gurdwara floors. They were my elders, my people, my community. I think of my Mom, my Dad, my family, my ancestors, and I think of myself—covered in blood, dead on the gurdwara floors.

Uncontrollable howling sounds of grief, pain, and agony start to pour out of my mouth. My body shakes and heaves on the couch as I wail. I can't even begin to explain, or understand, the depth of the anguish that's coming out of me.

The despair. The rage. The sadness. I'm overwhelmed in a way that's indescribable.

What I didn't know then but will learn over time is that my pain about the Oak Creek shooting, and other similar traumatic events, will evolve over the weeks, months, and years to follow. But it'll never fully go away. The tears, rage, guilt, sadness, and numbness will come and go like waves hitting a shore. My body will keep hurting, because trauma can keep hurting, especially when we still need to do our healing work. And being encased by systems built on hate, violence, and harm only make it worse.

As I lie on the couch crying for what feels like an eternity, the tears stop but the sobbing continues. I'm being reminded that there are many ways in which I hold hurt in my body.

TAKE A MOMENT TO REFLECT

What negative messages did you get from a young age about how to treat your body? How did this affect you? How does it show up for you today? How does it impact your sense of belonging?

As an adult, how have you been treating your body? Do you do the pinch test too? How do you judge your body?

You'll recall these words from this chapter: "When we neglect what we're feeling inside or we torment our body, we ultimately hurt our core self—our essence. And, in doing so, we stop belonging to ourselves." How have you seen this play out in your life?

What impact do traumatic events in society have on your body? How do you hold hurt inside you related to these experiences? Where does it show up in your body?

If you could change one or two things about how you treat or care for your body, what would that look like?

Questions for You to Explore Across All Chapters:

What are the key insights you've picked up from reading this chapter?

Which stories or messages most resonated with you? Why?

What are one or two things you'll do differently going forward?

CHAPTER SIX

TAKING OFF THE ADULT MASK AND ARMOR

Stevie Wonder has just finished belting out the last few words of "Overjoyed," but his band continues to softly play the melody. As he's been doing all evening between songs, he starts chatting with the thousands of us who are filling the sold-out stadium. My sister, Komal, and I have already decided that he's in a particularly soulful mood tonight, since he keeps talking about living a life rooted in purpose. I expected him to kill it musically, and he is, as he always does. What I didn't anticipate is that we'd also get a massive dose of insights on "how to live your best life." It feels a bit like being in a giant therapy session, and I'm all in. I didn't even realize how badly I've been needing these messages.

I'm in my early thirties, working hard on the 52nd floor of a Toronto skyscraper with my two besties: my Performing Self mask and my PPA armor. I'm making a salary that's more than my immigrant parents would've ever imagined, and on paper I'm living the "corporate dream." But my truth is very different: I've become a well-dressed, charming-on-the-outside, miserable-on-the-inside, parents-pleasing, single-and-lonely, exhausted-from-working, high-paid zombie.

So when Stevie launches into how being our true selves means everything when it comes to experiencing joy in life, my stomach drops. I immediately start to squirm in my seat while my eyes dart back and forth between the stage and the jumbo screen. I'm so flustered I don't even know where to look.

My sister clearly feels my energy shift, because in that exact moment she turns to me and asks, "Are you happy in your life?"

Like a champagne bottle that's been shaken and then uncorked, the weight of my pain starts to pour out of my eyes, nose, and heart. Between the tears and snot, I can barely bring myself to answer. But I don't have to. Komal already knows. She puts an arm around me and pulls me in close.

"It's okay," she whispers. "You're going to be okay."

I nod and take several breaths.

And right there, in the presence of Stevie Wonder, I vow to myself that I'm going to change my life. That I'm going to *choose* to live differently—which is what takes me to the ashram floor and leads me to commit to healing my trauma and wounds, being healthy, and, most importantly, finding belonging.

≡

As adults, we're projections of what happened to us when we were growing up. So, as kids, if we come to believe there's something wrong with us, the harmful effects of this will creep into every aspect of our adulthood—from our relationships to how we behave at work to how we treat ourselves.

But life can be even harder when we're older because it isn't just our elders who want us to meet their expectations. The "I disapprove of who you are" messaging hits us from across our family, lovers, friends, companions, professors, leaders, colleagues, bullies, frenemies, and even random strangers. The pressure to conform and mask can be so constant that we can be triggered to show up as our Performing Self with just about anyone. Not to mention, we also deal with a barrage of signals—which come at us both subtly and overtly—in society about what our identities represent and the rules we should therefore follow.

> This chapter talks about how your adult mask and armor can show up in any area of your life, and how you can start to move from hurting to healing in your journey to belong.

REALIZING WE NEED TO HEAL

Now that we're grown up and navigating a big wide world, anyone can push us to avert our spirits by how they treat us. It happens both knowingly and unknowingly, and it can feel relentless. We get direct verbal cues, like "You're not going to wear that, are you?!" and more subtle, nonverbal signals, like a raised eyebrow or loud sigh, which let us know we haven't shown up how they think we should. And since we so desperately want to belong in the complicated world of being an adult, our performances become more nuanced than when we were kids.

Sometimes we knowingly choose to perform—we deliberately take on a role. And other times, we don't have a clue we're doing this—our unconscious mind takes over to keep us safe. In *The Authenticity Principle*, I point out that we end up putting a mix of insights about ourselves out there, some of which is "either true, adapted but true, mostly true, somewhat true, you wish it were true, kinda sorta not really true, or so totally not true." We do things we don't even enjoy to impress people who don't care about us. For example, we change how we speak so that others will take us more seriously even though we hate doing it. We go to unending lengths to do things to our bodies so that people will think we're beautiful. We put on a sunshine smile even though we're dying inside. And we double down on acting as though our life is only beautiful and never hard.

> " There may even be moments where performing will feel worth it, but then something will remind us about how soul crushing it is to let others control us and put out our spark.

And here's the thing: it makes sense that we do this as adults. We want to guard our hearts. So, for many of us, as part of our Performing Self, we think we *need* to crank up our positivity-perfection-achievement several notches. If we can act like our life is happy-happy and flawless, and that we're always winning, then maybe others won't take their love away or hurt us. If this stings as a child, it can slash even more as an adult.

Regardless, at the end of the day, performing sucks, whether we're kids or adults. It doesn't reflect who we really are; it masks what we're actually feeling and thinking, and it pushes down how we truly want to behave. Because of this, it's exhausting to do. At times we'll feel sick to our stomach while doing it. In other moments, it'll feel like we can't breathe. We'll even fill with so much shame while we're doing it that we can't stop self-flogging. And here's a big takeaway: there may even be moments where performing will feel worth it, but then something will remind us about how soul crushing it is to let others control us and put out our spark.

As I entered my adulthood, I knew I wasn't okay. I could tell my soul was hurting. I was nursing the wounds from my childhood and teenage years. I wanted to soar, but I couldn't get myself to fly. My wings were being clipped by my childhood trauma.

And I knew I needed to do something.

$$\equiv$$

It's 3:55 p.m. and I have five minutes to make it to the common room on my coed university residence floor.

I'm bustling to get there because I need to claim the TV to watch *The Oprah Winfrey Show*, which will be on at 4:00 p.m. for an hour. *The Young and the Restless* airs at 4:30 p.m., and if I don't get there now and take over the remote control, I'll lose my window. Some of the girls on my floor love this soap and will flood the room very shortly. If I've already captured the remote, they're going to have to join me. Meanwhile, the boys on our floor will avoid this room like the plague for hours.

Watching *Oprah* religiously is a practice I've brought with me to college from high school. When I was still living at home, I'd curl up every Monday to

Friday during this time slot to soak in what the queen and her healing experts had to say about living and being your best. I'm still doing this now because, well, I desperately need it. I'm twenty years old, but I can tell I've brought my need to perform from my childhood into my adulthood. I'm just at the tip of understanding how badly hurt I am from all that's happened to me.

Hanging out with Oprah and her guests has become my salvation. It's the mid-nineties, and I'm still leaps and bounds away from using the internet to help me explore my issues. This is the best I've got. And it's helping me a lot.

Watching a diverse range of people be vulnerable and talk about how they're in pain, almost on a daily basis, is planting a seed that I'm not inherently flawed. I'm not the only one who's armed herself with a mask, armor, and stage in the pursuit of belonging—in fact, I'm picking up this is a phenomenon. I'm realizing that feeling wounded is normal, and so is talking about it. And the buzzing sensation I've been feeling in my body for years now that screams "I'm experiencing injustice" is warranted. I deserve better and more. I know this to be true. I just didn't know how to make this happen. Until now.

Several times now, I've heard Oprah and her guests basically say that they felt a spark inside them while they were growing up and knew they were destined for more than what was coming their way. I always drink up these words. It's like they're giving me permission to feel the same. And so, the fire in me is starting to build.

I make it to the common room at 3:59 p.m., and no one is in sight. I dive for the remote before anyone can appear. Still standing, I click through the channels just in time to catch the show's theme song. I exhale in relief as I snuggle into the sofa. For the next hour, I'm home.

$$\equiv$$

The hours of taking in pearls of wisdom on belonging from Oprah and her guests inspired me to move from a place of constantly hurting into committing to healing and building my core wisdom. It opened the door to life change when I both needed it and was willing to take whatever help I could get. From watching the healing experts on the screen, I turned to devouring all kinds of self-help books. Poring through the pages, I began to understand that who I am as an adult is a reflection of my childhood. My heart was starting to feel how deeply my inner child—Sweet, Soft Little Ritu—was in pain because of the viciousness of the bullying I experienced and from the cultural tension in how I was parented. But I was also learning that I could devote time to caring for her wounds and mine—that there were actual practices I could use to help me.

On top of gobbling up Oprah's messages and self-help books, I began to take more social science classes in college, where I dove into research, theories, and frameworks on the "why" behind what happens to us in life. This is where I came to see there are systems in society that've intentionally been designed to hold us back and prevent us from belonging. That we're not the problem, nor are we broken—instead, these deliberate structures are created in such a way to hate on us and make us hate on ourselves.

It also started to sink in that, given many of my identities and their intersection, hate was unfortunately going to continue to come my way, and it would serve me to get ahead of it. I needed hands-on help to do this, which is what led me to begin doing psychotherapy (an experience that continues today). As I made my way through school and into the work world, therapy was a constant, even though I told next to no one I was doing it. Many people back then (and now, *hello*!) held the flawed belief that only really messed-up people go to therapists, and I didn't want to be seen that way. But as we dug deep into uncovering and tending to Little Ritu's and Grown-Up Ritu's wounds, therapy changed my world.

I constantly thank the Universe that I made the decision to begin therapy when I did, because I had no idea what was waiting for me when I started working within the bastions of corporate elitism. The messages of "Don't be you, be like us!" and "Conform! Conform! Conform!" were omnipresent. If I thought dealing with bullying and strict parenting was tough, little did I know that I was jumping from one fire into another.

FITTING IN VS. ACTUAL BELONGING

To survive working in the corporate skyscrapers for a decade, I had to give Oscar-worthy performances left, right, and center. Only I didn't have an inkling of the depth to which I was doing this back then. But I sure do now: I wore so much navy and gray even though Punjabi culture basically doesn't view these as colors, and nor do I; I kept my hair short because it was deemed "more professional"; I developed Ritu-the-Lawyer-Speak, which reflected the King's English, and After-Hours-Ritu-Speak, which was filled with slang and my favorite thing to say of all time, the F-word; I'd drop the pitch of my voice to be lower, and I'd speak slower so that I'd sound more like a man; and I held back all signs of tears and sadness, even though I often felt like wailing at work—all as a way to be accepted, to get ahead, and to deflect judgment in the hardcore, cutthroat, White male-dominated corporate world.

And there's still more.

My Performing Self threw herself into social stuff that bored me to tears, but I thought would help me to be seen as one of the "good ones." I went to the opera and symphony, where I'd play the game of counting all the people who didn't look White to me; I went to so many hockey games in ice-cold arenas, I almost froze to death; I snored my way through golf lessons and nearly shattered into a million pieces while learning how to ski; and I attended so many wine-and-cheese gatherings in colonial-style mahogany- and tapestry-filled rooms that I thought I'd crack from the dullness.

If that wasn't enough, then there was my PPA armor! I masterfully curated a bubbly, chipper, and almost-flawless persona that I thought was helping me to hide my feelings of self-doubt and being an impostor. If I could just be excellent-excellent-excellent on every single thing by focusing on achieve-achieve-achieve, then maybe others wouldn't find out that I was a fraud. Or they'd stop hating on me. Or they'd give me the opportunities I rightfully deserved. Or they'd properly reward me for my brilliance and I'd make my parents proud. Or they'd finally give me room to just be who I wanted to be. And maybe then I'd feel a sense of belonging.

> " Performing to fit in will never take the place of actual belonging. When we change who we are or what we want to meet other people's expectations of us, they get to decide our joy and, in doing so, we give away our power.

It was so much. Too much.

Since I was focused on performing all day long, it was awfully hard to step out of these roles at night when I was spending time with my family, partying with friends, and trying to meet husband candidates. I was flailing across relationships: I was trying to detach myself from the codependent dynamic I now had with my parents by drawing new boundaries, which wasn't going well; I was hanging out with a friend crew that I felt really disconnected from but I feared breaking up with because I didn't want to be lonely, even though I already was; and I was making toxic choices in my dating life and constantly feeling heartbroken.

But here's something fascinating: while I was overriding the "I'm so miserable" thoughts in my head, my body was letting me know that I was hurting. My sleep quality and quantity were a wreck, and I always felt exhausted. I cracked a tooth from clenching my jaw so hard at night while sleeping. I constantly had a "party in my stomach," which is what I came to call the gurgly and bloated feeling I used to have in my belly nonstop. And I wanted to cry or scream or do both at once all the time.

It was when the intense lower back pain started, and I was in excruciating pain, that I finally started to understand that my body was screaming "STOP!" In so many ways, it was telling me to slow down, tune in, and take a look at how unanchored and unhappy I was.

This is how yoga and meditation finally came into my life as a way of being. From taking weekly classes to ease my back pain and release some of my stress, I moved on to squeezing yoga workshops and wellness retreats into my wild work schedule. But that still didn't feel like enough. Because I could see my life needed to be gutted, I decided to take a three-month sabbatical from my law firm job, and I escaped to the South Indian ashram to study the philosophy of yoga.

The winds of change were about to sweep me up and take my spirit to places I had only heard about. In *The Authenticity Principle*, I wrote: "Through belonging, we experience feelings of acceptance, love, connection, meaning, purpose, inclusion, kinship, and more. But belonging actually isn't about fitting in, which some of us mistakenly believe it to be—it's about being accepted for who we are." What I was getting at here is that we must choose to be surrounded by people who love and accept us for our authenticity. That's where true belonging lives versus when we feel pressure to mask or armor.

This is a key life lesson I absorbed while I was at the ashram, which we'll explore more in *Healing*: performing to fit in will never take the place of actual belonging. When we change who we are or what we want to meet other people's expectations of us, they get to decide our joy and, in doing so, we give away our power.

Don't let anyone steal your spark.

=

I smooth out the ripples across the front of my pink-and-red floral dress. (Thankfully I'm joyously breaking the childhood promise I made to never "clash," especially when I'm doing photoshoots and speaking on global stages.) It took me about fourteen tries to zip the dress up in the back on my own, and even my history of clothing contortionism didn't help. I considered going down to the hotel lobby to ask for help, but the vision of people looking at me funny took me to dark places.

I know I need to get a move on. While I'm almost always late for everything in life given that Indian Standard Time (I.S.T.) was also part of my upbringing, I never mess around with being tardy for a speaking gig. Especially not for something as big as today's event, where very shortly I'll be on the conference center stage keynoting for an hour in front of a few thousand people.

I strap a thin, black, shiny belt around my waist. This is an essential accessory when I'm wearing a dress to present. You'll never see me without one. I need to latch the microphone pack onto something. And the chunky gold necklaces I've become known for wearing when I'm speaking, I need them too—often to dangle the head of the microphone. Even when it comes to audio technology, I'm reminded that the world is designed for men, White men in particular.

I carefully apply bright-red lipstick while standing before the mirror. I do my best to not go over the lip line, and then step back to check myself out.

"Well done, Ritu Bhasin!" I say out loud. "Looking good."

I'm almost ready. For the final touch, I grab the red felt shoe bag from my suitcase and pull out the pair of round-toed black patent leather red-bottom heels. I instantly notice a smudge on the left shoe and start to fixate on removing it. I haven't forgotten my privilege. I know these heels cost more than some people's monthly rent payment. When I first told Papa Bhasin how much I forked over for these heels, he was shocked. "You paid what?! You know how much I paid for these shoes?" he asked, gesturing to his feet. "Twenty-five dollars at Walmart!" he happily declared.

Despite being the beneficiary of our fancy gifts, my Dad is still delighted to wear the bargains he hunts down. It's all good. I know he's secretly proud as an immigrant father that these are his Putri's speaker heels. But he's not the only one who's grateful. I am, too, for I know what it took to walk in these shoes.

As I carefully step into the heels, my mind drifts to when I was twelve years old. Suddenly, Tretorns had become all the rage with The Mean Crew. All around me, they were sporting the white canvas tennis sneakers with the green U-shaped logo. And, because I wanted to be one of them, I needed Tretorns too. Of course, when I asked my parents to spend the hundred dollars it would take for me to prance around in them, my request was quickly denied. Instead, Mama Bhasin took me to Woolco and bought me similarly shaped white cloth sneakers that cost $4.99. I should have just left them as they were. But my creative juices started to flow the moment I got them home.

While I couldn't have the real ones, I could turn these into Tretorns. For the next few days, I spent hours staring at the cool kids' feet at school trying to memorize the design. Then, when I was ready to set free my inner da Vinci, I took a marker to my new sneakers, doing my best to draw on the U-shape, and voila! I had a homemade pair of Tretorns.

I thought I had created genius. My parents certainly did not feel the same way. But more importantly, nor did The Mean Crew. It unleashed unspeakable amounts of mockery. I can even remember thinking to myself, "One day, will people still laugh at me?"

I'm now standing on stage with a few thousand sets of eyes staring at me in my floral dress and red-bottom shoes. I'm no longer "acting" Ritu. I'm just *being* Ritu. And, as I flail my arms, and I go on in my super-loud and sometimes high-pitched voice, people are still laughing.

But this time, it's with me and not at me.

TAKE A MOMENT TO REFLECT

What disapproving messages have come your way about who you are as an adult? How do these messages affect you? What's the impact on your sense of belonging?

In this chapter, I write "performing to fit in will never take the place of actual belonging." How do you mask and armor to "fit in," if at all? How does this affect your spirit? What would actual belonging look like for you?

When you're clocking the pressure to perform, what does it feel like in your body? What sensations and feelings come up inside you? Where in your body do you carry hurt or tension? What thoughts go through your mind?

What experiences have helped you to become open to self-care and wellness practices? Why are these practices important for your journey to belong? What else do you want to do to care for yourself going forward?

Questions for You to Explore Across All Chapters:

What are the key insights you've picked up from reading this chapter?

Which stories or messages most resonated with you? Why?

What are one or two things you'll do differently going forward?

HEALING

CHAPTER SEVEN

A NEW PARADIGM FOR HEALING

The pounding startles me. This is the third time it's happened in the last few days.

It feels like someone is tapping their fist, knuckles first, smack dab in the middle of my chest, right between my boobs, near my heart. The throbbing started softly but has picked up in intensity.

The first time it happened, I was meditating in the ashram's main hall during the morning satsang. The second time it happened, I was chanting along in evening satsang. This time I'm lying in Shavasana with my eyes closed on the hall's floor, on top of my cheap-o mat, at the end of an asana class.

I open my left eye to see if someone is there. Nope, no one is hovering over me knocking on my chest like it's a door. No one was there during the satsangs either. I close my eye. The drumming continues. "Is this a build-up to a heart attack?!" I ask myself as a vision of the news headline "Punjabi-Canadian Woman Dies of a Heart Attack in South Indian Ashram" flashes through my mind.

Don't be so dramatic, Ritu. Calm yourself. You know what to do.

And with that, as I've been taught to do in our pranayama lessons, I start to deepen my breathing by driving my inhalations down into the bottom of my lungs, causing my diaphragm to contract and my belly area to push out. On my even slower exhalations, I do the opposite.

I've been at the ashram for two weeks now for the teachers' training program, and it's been a whirlwind of change. I can't imagine what the next bit will bring. I now have a settled routine, which is worlds apart from how I've been living in Toronto. I'm up every morning by 5:30 a.m. to be on time for the morning satsang, where we meditate and chant, starting at 6:00 a.m. The day continues with a mix of classes on asana practice, pranayama, yoga theory, the Bhagavad Gita, and kirtan, and ends with an evening satsang. Squeezed into the schedule are just two veggie meals a day, which remarkably leave me satiated.

There's so much packed into each day, it feels like we don't have a second to just chill—and to get our yoga teacher certificate, we can't skip out on anything. But even though it's a whirlwind, it's amazing how much more I enjoy it than my life back home. I've even become used to wearing the yellow t-shirt and white pants daily. I have a good cleaning sequence going now: I wear one set of the uniform for two days, then wash it in the twenty minutes I have between the morning meal and my slot for ashram chores. Maintaining a morning laundry time is best so that I can use the afternoon sun to dry everything off. It's fascinating to think about the lengths I go to in my real life to dry clothes in such a way that yields fluffy softness. But here, the crunch-crunch of my sundried outfits feels fine.

What I've experienced these last few weeks—and how I've handled it—is affirming I'm more flexible and adaptable than I thought I was. And it's also unlocking all kinds of awareness of what's happening in my body, which is fundamental to growing my core wisdom. I'm starting to sense things that I've never noticed, or paid attention to, before—like a buzzing feeling in my lower back and tingling on my face. Not to mention that because I'm starting to pry off the corners of my Performing Self mask and PPA armor, I'm clocking powerful effects like a pounding sensation in my chest area. Which continues as I lie here in Shavasana with my eyes closed.

Despite my deep breathing, the tapping won't stop. And now, the tears are starting.

This is a new addition; the tears didn't happen the first two times. I can feel the wetness dripping down both sides of my face and into each of my ears. I didn't realize tears can still fall when your eyes are shut. I'm learning so much all at once. I can tell my body wants to let go and sob wildly, but I can also hear The Voice commanding, *No! Now is not the time! Don't you dare open those floodgates!* Except that my body may not be able to listen to my inner saboteur, as I can sense I'm on the brink of an explosion of tears. I'm going back and forth with the "Do I or don't I?!," plus the pounding is getting even more intense, and it's all happening so quickly...

Then, suddenly, I hear the voice of our South Indian asana instructor inviting us to bring our attention back into the room and start to wiggle our fingers and toes.

And just like that, in tandem, both the tears and the tapping stop.

I start to follow his cues, slowly making my way to a seated position at the front of my mat. He brings us into a chant to close our asana practice. I've done this chant several times now since arriving at the ashram, but today it feels extra long. He says a few things about the afternoon's lesson, and then he lets us go for our morning meal. But I can't bring myself to get up. The tears are still there somewhere, as is the concern about the throbbing.

"Talk to Swami Ji," I tell myself. "He may be able to help you." Before The Voice can talk me out of it, I find myself standing in front of my tall, graceful teacher at the front of the hall. As I open my mouth to speak, the tears start again. I tell him about the drumming I've been feeling in my chest area, and all the emotion that's been coming up, and how I don't understand it.

As I speak and cry, he looks at me tenderly, nodding his head as he listens. When I'm finally done, we stand there in silence for a bit. Then, he cocks his head to one side and offers me this pearl of wisdom: "Ritu, energy is moving in your body. When the heart gets hurt, we can have a block there. In your heart chakra, you have a blockage."

"Oh, Swami Ji, you have no idea how badly my heart has been hurting and for how long," I say to myself.

He continues with this next pearl of wisdom, which speaks directly to the importance of developing our core wisdom. "It's moving now. Let it move. Don't stop it. You'll also feel other things move. Just let it happen."

I'm sobbing now. I had no idea this is what's been happening inside me.

He nods his head and smiles. "You'll be fine, Ritu," he says, offering another pearl. "Your body is healing. And this is what healing looks like."

My mind is blown. I had never thought of healing in this way before.

Through the tears, I nod back, sniffle, take a big breath in and sigh it out through my mouth. I needed this.

$$=$$

As I talked about in *Hurting*, given all we go through in life, it makes sense that many of us continue to hold hurt in our bodies and can sense that our minds are riddled with negativity. The saving grace is that we can move forward from what's happened to us by doing the deep self-work that helps us to let go of our pain. To make this happen, we need to do three important things:

- Prioritize our healing journey
- Embrace a new healing mindset
- Reframe how we feel about the ancient healing practices rooted in our cultures

Prioritizing your healing journey can be an immediate, dramatic shift within you where you realize healing is everything and you're going to work to make it happen. Or it can be a slower journey of change that bit by bit moves how you take care of yourself. You can also flow somewhere between these two ends. Whichever path you take, you will feel the craving inside you to thrive, and this is what will lead you to change how you feel, act, emote, think, speak, and dress, so that you can belong. While this work can feel exhausting and endless, at the end of the day you want to do it because you deserve to live a really good life, one where you belong, and not just cope during your years on this Earth.

Embracing a new healing mindset means adjusting your current thinking to center your body and body-based practices when you're taking care of yourself. It's about understanding healing isn't just about focusing on your mind to purge negative thoughts. It's about spending more time focusing on the hurt you're carrying in your body, especially if you've turned your nose up at this in the past, which I'll admit I have. This is why you'll want to come to rely on your core wisdom—the knowledge you hold within that leads you to tune in to and understand what your body and mind are signaling and moves you to care for yourself.

Reframing how you feel about ancient healing practices is about adopting ancestral strategies for being well. Rather than shunning these strategies, you're starting to rely on them to help shed your pain, be more resilient, and live a healthy life. This awakening to ancient healing practices is something I haven't touched on yet, and it's what we'll explore first in *Healing*.

> This chapter digs into why it's important to prioritize taking care of yourself using ancient, ancestral body-based healing practices along your path to belonging.

OUR ANCESTORS KNEW

Growing up, I was quite a sickly child. From stomach issues and tonsillitis to fevers and cold sores, I was unwell all the time. I even had the chickenpox twice, which is extremely rare but possible, and both times were severe cases. As a kid, I didn't have the wherewithal to connect these health issues with the stress I was experiencing, but it makes sense to me now.

My poor parents! They were constantly concerned about me and my siblings, given all the maladies that circulated among us, and "feel better" therapies became a huge focus in our upbringing. Of course, since I grew up in a quintessential Punjabi immigrant-run household, it should come as no surprise they focused on natural remedies for any and every health issue where healing was required.

Body tension? We didn't need to worry! Surely there was a yoga asana that could help. But also, back in the eighties and nineties, Mama and Papa Bhasin were early adopters of the new at-home massage technologies and had us covered with an array of aids to release and settle the tension in our body: back massagers, foot massagers, circulation devices, and electric-current-thingys that would send shooting pulses throughout the body. Then there were the homemade apparatuses: tennis balls in socks, straps to contort ourselves, and heating pads in multiple shapes and sizes for any area. In fact, eighty-plus-year-old Papa Bhasin still makes heating bags, stitched using colorful fabrics and filled with rice, to gift to family, friends, and strangers. Adorable, I know.

Feeling down or stressed? My parents would press "play" on the tape recorder, and kirtan music would bring peaceful, centering energy into our chaotic household. And if that wasn't enough, Mama Bhasin would happily demonstrate a range of pranayama practices we could use to calm the hell down, including rapidly pumping the belly in and out (Kapalabhati) and taking turns closing either nostril (Nadi Shodhana).

Earache? My Dad would bring out a small blue plastic bottle that was at least four hundred years old, covered in a masking tape label on which he'd written "EAR" in black pen. It likely held medicated eye drops once upon a time, but it was now the home for an oil concoction he'd cooked up. We'd get a few drops in each ear before bedtime and, like magic, our issues would be resolved within a few days.

Sore throat and cough? My Mom would pull out a few tins from the cupboard that held potent dried leaves and spices. Then she'd boil them into what felt like a poisonous elixir we'd have to chug down, and, if we complained, we got more. This would be followed by a warmed-up oil rub Mama Bhasin made that she'd furiously knead into our neck and throat region.

Stuffed-up nose? Lucky us, we got to flush out our nostrils using a neti (correct pronunciation: nee-thee) pot filled with warm salt water. The process was simple enough: we'd tilt our head to the left first; pour liquid into the right nostril; rapidly blow out our nose; watch the water and snot fly out; and then repeat this procedure on the left nostril. It felt like the grossest thing ever.

Speaking of gross... Tummy ache? We had the pleasure of taking Hajmola, infamous Ayurvedic digestion tablets that are from Mother India. But, as kiddies, we called them "tuthee golees" (the "s" on the end of golee makes it a mash-up of Punjabi and English), which translates to "poo pills" because they literally smelled like... well, poo.

Looking back, what couldn't be healed by a natural technique, potion, tonic, mixture, or ointment straight from the motherland or created from ingredients taken from the Bhasin Family apothecary cupboards?!

Many of us come from ancient cultures that have *centuries* of experience with natural healing and body- and mind-based strategies for managing our physical, mental, and spiritual health and wellness. Our ancestors from every corner of the world relied on the Earth's soil, plants, vegetation, herbs, animals, stones, and more, and on the human body and mind itself, to help them heal and be well. We may have mocked these skill sets as kids, but as adults I hope we can now see how extraordinary this is.

If you take a step back to think about the magnitude and power of what our cultures created and contributed to the world, it's magical and profound. Thousands of years ago, they invented transformative technologies, practices, and traditions for healing and wellness in the face of life hardships, and, of course, they had it right. I'm thinking about meditation, yoga, pranayama, Ayurveda, plant medicines, fasting and other body-cleansing exercises, massage, Reiki, tai chi, qigong, capoeira, gatka, acupuncture, cupping, naturopathic medicine, bodywork practices, rhythm-focused rituals like drumming, dancing, and chanting, and many, many more.

> " If you take a step back to think about the magnitude and power of what our cultures created and contributed to the world, it's magical and profound.

I could go on, but the point is clear. Our ancestors were amazing. So let this be a takeaway for all of us going forward: We must revel in this truth. Because it's truly genius. But I'll be the first to admit that it's taken me ages to finally see this.

≡

"Have you tried psyllium husk?" my girlfriend asks me. I immediately look up and stare into her bright-blue eyes that are sparkling against her milky-white skin. "I swear by it!"

While it feels a bit "TMI," I've just opened up to my friend about all the digestive troubles I've had for years now, given that she can relate. I'm in my mid-thirties, as is she, but I've been battling tummy problems since I was a kid. When I was younger, it was an issue of being clogged up all the time. But for the last several years, it's switched over to the opposite end of the spectrum where I'm having all kinds of wild "parties in my stomach." I constantly feel gurgly and bloated and, while I'm eating lots, it's often like my meals go in one end and immediately come out the other.

I've been poked for food allergies and intolerances, I've been prodded for celiac and other diseases, and I've done all kinds of elimination diets, but nothing seems to work. Carrying around probiotics, activated charcoal, and Pepto pills has become the Band-Aid solution to this never-ending plague, which is properly disrupting my life. I'm always on alert, worrying about when the next "party" will start, because it hits in the most inopportune of times. Like when I'm in a boardroom for a meeting or on a date or on the dancefloor at a nightclub. It's the worst because, on top of the discomfort, broadcasting the unexpected party that's now taking place in my stomach is not my jam.

I don't know this yet, and if you were to tell me now I wouldn't believe you anyway, but a time is coming when these issues will largely go away and I will be fine. The changes will be rooted in the healing work I have yet to dig more deeply into, which includes practices directly tied back to what my ancestors would have done. The moment is coming soon, and, when it does, it will transform my world. But, at this point, I still haven't cracked the code.

"You take psyllium husk?!" I ask her incredulously. "My Dad's been telling me to do this for years and years now. He learned to do this when he was growing up in India. He says it even helps with overactive systems, like mine."

"I sure do," she replies. "I even go to an Indian grocery store to buy the brand with the green box."

I know exactly what she's talking about. I can see my Dad pulling the green box out of the kitchen cupboard of our family home and booming loudly, "This Isabgol is the best!" Except that when he tells me to do it, I roll my eyes and run for the hills. I'm still rejecting a lot of the natural remedies he and Mama Bhasin are bringing my way. Why? Because I think they're "weird." I still haven't fully opened my heart to their ancient ways of doing things unless the practices have become mainstream in Americanized culture.

I have no idea that one day, Papa Bhasin will be my primary Isabgol supplier and I'll have stacks of the green boxes in my cupboard. I'll need them for my daily morning routine of taking a spoonful of Isabgol with a glass of warm water. It'll be one more thing I'll do to help my body feel better. But what'll get me there initially won't be my father and all his brilliant untapped wisdom. It'll be my blue-eyed friend with her milky white skin who'll inspire me to do it.

Over time, I'll come to see that my rejection of South Asian wellness and healing practices directly connects with learning to hate both myself and my cultural roots while growing up. I'll also clock that, at every turn in society, I continue to receive these oppressive types of messages. Which is another reason why my core wisdom will increasingly become my anchor in life.

EMBRACING OUR ROOTS

Given all the hate that we feel around us, it's not surprising some of us ended up rejecting our ancestors' healing practices. But as part of our journey to live better, we must interrupt and reframe how we look at the natural healing technologies our ancestors created for managing health and wellness—especially as it relates to shedding the hurt we carry from the hardships we encounter along our path to belonging.

In my twenties and early thirties, to help my body and mind heal from the pain I was bearing, I turned to what I saw around me: I threw myself into doing psychotherapy, reading self-help books, journaling, going on weekend relaxation retreats, and more. But when this combination of self-care practices wasn't getting at what I ultimately needed to heal, I *still* didn't reach for the ancient practices my ancestors created. I continued to be largely closed off to them, because I learned to hate our traditions.

" As part of our journey to live better, we must interrupt and reframe how we look at the natural healing technologies our ancestors created for managing health and wellness.

Traditional rituals rooted in nature, sound, movement, meditation, mindfulness, deep breathing, and more are *exactly* what we need to help heal the wounds caused by the hurtful, hateful, and harmful things we've experienced. By getting to the heart of the hurt that lives in our body, our ancestral practices directly help us to settle our nervous system when it becomes activated; release trauma-related energy; let go of difficult sensations, emotions, and thoughts; minimize the physical and mental pain we're holding; and interrupt the negative narratives that are racing through our mind.

This is why we need to recast how we look at our respective ancestral technologies. It's through these types of practices we heal and unlock our ability to thrive, flourish, be well, grow, and shine. By committing to doing them, we grow the wings we need to soar.

We begin to let go of our feelings of unworthiness.

We sense greater anchoring, calmness, and peace within us.

We become healthier—physically, mentally, and spiritually.

We feel more alive, inspired, and present.

We feel freer to be authentic in how we live.

We use our voice to speak our truth.

We experience renewed purpose and meaning in life.

We stand in our power more often.

We no longer avert our eyes.

We rise.

We belong.

All this is possible by embracing what our ancestors knew would keep us healthy and whole. This is what healing is all about and why it's so important.

" While this work can feel exhausting and endless, at the end of the day you want to do it because you deserve to live a really good life, one where you belong, and not just cope during your years on this Earth.

≡

We're an hour into my deep-dive workshop on the importance of cultural competence for inclusive leadership. I'm standing at the front of the boardroom facing a long wooden table, around which twenty corporate executives are sitting. I've just kicked off another group exercise. I've asked them to name some of the biases they hold about behaviors in the workplace that are culturally different from what they're used to.

I love holding reflection discussions like this because it gives me a window into people's lives—in this case, how a custom in one culture is worshipped, while in another, the same custom is vilified. Basically, it's like I'm running a giant research study across my presentations, and I love it.

I call on someone whose hand is up. "Yes?" I say, smiling and nodding.

"I've noticed that sometimes, in the women's washroom, people will openly blow their nose right into the sink, one nostril at a time, instead of using a tissue," she shares. "I know it's probably bad to say this, but I'm really turned off by it."

I pause for a moment and consider what to say. As I go back and forth in my mind, the *Jeopardy!* theme song might as well be playing.

The thing is, that very morning I did a variation of this to help purge the snot related to my bad seasonal allergies. This was after I meditated and did some of the pranayama I learned from my Mom and at the ashram, but before I ate a spoonful of Isabgol, the way my Dad has now taught me to take it. And now I'm dithering about how personal to be.

I decide to be straight up, which is usually where I go these days. First, I explain how common a practice this is for many people from cultures around the world—and not just in the comfort of their homes, but in public washrooms too. Then I talk about how I also used to be grossed out by all nose-blowing activities back in the day, even when done at home privately, and sometimes still am depending on what it is. But now, as part of embracing my cultural practices, I'm pro-empty-out-your-nose, even though I'm sometimes repulsed by the outcome. I go on to share with her and all the other leaders in the room that I neti-ed that very morning, which involves blowing my nose into the sink instead of a tissue. I get in to how I did it using a neti pot I'd picked up at the ashram, why it's so good for me to do this, and that I highly recommend they try it. I then talk about what to do when you feel the zap of I-don't-like-you-because-you-put-your-snot-into-the-work-sink energy go through your body about a teammate, a skill I've been working on developing and that's helped me in similar moments.

After my session is done, as I walk out of the building, the following thought goes through my mind: in my forty-plus years on this planet, I never thought that one day I'd stand in the hallowed halls of a famous company and talk about how I regularly clear snot out of my nose as part of my healing practices.

But that's what just happened. On my journey to experience belonging as much as I can, I'm happily cleaning my nose out using Indian practices, I'm openly talking about it in the most unexpected of places, and I'm bursting with pride that this ancient tradition of my people carries on.

Bring on more healing.

TAKE A MOMENT TO REFLECT

Prior to reading this chapter, what was your mindset about healing from the hurtful experiences you've had along your life's journey? Were you connecting healing with your journey to belong?

To what extent have you been prioritizing your healing?

When growing up, what traditional healing practices did your elders push on you? How did you react to them back then? How do you feel about them now?

How can you use your ancestors' healing practices to help you experience greater belonging? What practices come to mind that you'd like to start leveraging right away?

What mindset will you embrace going forward about healing? What will you do to care for yourself?

Questions for You to Explore Across All Chapters:

What are the key insights you've picked up from reading this chapter?

Which stories or messages most resonated with you? Why?

What are one or two things you'll do differently going forward?

CHAPTER EIGHT

THE MAGIC AND POWER OF CORE WISDOM

The vacuum crashes into the door frame as I push it into my parents' bedroom. It's followed by a stuttering noise.

"Oh frog!" I say out loud, and then quickly look behind me to check if Papa Bhasin has seen this go down.

I can hear him down the hall, but he's not in view. Relief washes over me. The "Don't touch the walls!" messaging from my childhood rushes through my mind. He'd turn six shades of purple when we'd ding the paint and make a mark, and he still does. The annoying thing is that I've now become my father. You should see me glare at guests as they hover near the walls of my home.

I'm here for an afternoon visit. It's been a few weeks since we moved Mama to a nursing home because of the need for full-time care as the Alzheimer's disease progresses during the pandemic. To say we're all heartbroken would be an understatement. It feels like my heart has been slashed and the grief is uncontrollably pouring out. I can't even wrap my mind around how hard it is for my Dad to have his wife of almost fifty years move out of the home they recently bought to enjoy during their last years together. I can feel the anguish in his energy and see it in the look on his face.

As Ritu Bhenji, I wish I could wave a magic wand and take away his sadness, and I do try. But, of course, it doesn't work. He needs to mourn his own loss, as I do mine. So, instead, I find a suitable alternate response that's fitting by Indian standards: I offer to do chores. He begrudgingly takes me up on it, and I get why. I'm lousy at this. While I was essentially a professional chore-doer as a child, I hated every minute of it. And now as an adult, I'm allergic to doing anything domestic, so I usually do a shoddy job. Lucky Santosh.

Remarkably though, I'm finding vacuuming to be very relaxing today. Door banging aside, I have a rhythm going as I daydream along the way. It feels meditative, which is a reminder that I don't need to be on the ashram floor to connect with myself.

Pulling the vacuum close to the walk-in closet, I turn on the light. I'm about to enter when I catch a glimpse of a handful of Mama Bhasin's sweaters dangling from the clothing rod. They're mostly in shades of lilac, the color she's become attached to as the dementia has increasingly taken hold. And because my Dad is obsessed with cleanliness and order, the shoulders are perfectly aligned and equidistant as they hang neatly on her side.

We decided to pack only some of her clothes to take to the nursing home, and this is what remains. Looking at them now is a reminder that she's gone from their house and won't ever be back. I feel an intense wave of agony jolt through me, starting in my stomach area and then making its way up my chest. Tears fill my eyes, and an aching cry wants to leave my lips.

But before I can let any of this out, I hear my Dad call out, "Putri? Putri?" as the sound of his voice gets closer and closer. I worry if he sees me cry, his heart will hurt even more, and I can't bear this thought. Thankfully, The Voice jumps in, right on time: *No, don't do this, not right now. It'll upset your Dad. Save it for later.* And in a split second, I push back the tears, close my mouth, and put a toothless grin on my face, putting someone else's needs before my own. I override my body's natural, automatic desire to let out its grief at the sight of the shades of lilac.

I do this despite knowing from my trauma and wellness studies that healing isn't just about sensing what's happening within us, it's about instinctively discharging the energy that comes up to help settle ourselves. If my body is telling me to sob and shake and twitch because I'm feeling upset by the sight of Mama's sweaters, and what this symbolizes, then it's important I honor that. Over time, I want my body to get used to releasing what's naturally coming up inside me, because this will help me to build a more regulated and resilient nervous system—one that's less easily activated. Not to mention, it'll help me to manage the negative thoughts that dance in my head.

However, in this very minute, I'm just a girl who's overcome with grief and wants to protect her Dad. My PPA armor is still dangling off me, emotional exhaustion fills my entire being, and I'm struggling with how to hold space for both myself and my father right now. I just don't have it in me to unravel.

I do want to live better. I'm committed to doing the work. Because, when it comes to healing, I know that every step we take helps. And so, this is what'll push me, later in the evening when I'm back home, to put on kirtan music, lie down on my couch, and take my body and mind back to the closet and the sweaters. As the pangs of heartache immediately come back up, I'll freely wail and tremble with my face against the soft, furry couch. And as I do this, I'll keep breathing deeply while switching back and forth between hugging myself and putting my hand on my heart chakra, where years back I felt the tapping. I'll just let out whatever comes up. And it'll feel both beautiful and hard to do.

But in this moment, I can't. And that's totally fine.

Standing in the closet in front of the lilac sweaters, with the vacuum purring away and my heart still beating quickly, I hear my Dad's voice summoning me to finish up vacuuming, so that we can eat the dhal chawal he's made.

"Yes, Dadda," I yell loudly over the sound of the vacuum. "I'm coming."

≡

Because we literally carry hurt in our bodies, our healing work is vital. This is exactly why we want to develop our *core wisdom*—the knowing that lives inside us that leads us to track and settle the sensations, feelings, and thoughts we're holding, and to understand intimately what our body and mind are signaling.

Our core wisdom knows we must be both embodied—focused on our body—and intentional—focused on our mind—so that our healing journey is holistic and balanced. In targeting both the body and mind, core wisdom is what mindfulness is all about—gaining awareness of what we're sensing, feeling, and thinking within us in any given moment, and doing this in a non-judgmental way.

> This chapter highlights the importance of growing your core wisdom for your healing journey, and how to make that happen—all to help you experience greater belonging.

BREAKING DOWN THE HEALING POWER OF CORE WISDOM

Core wisdom is the knowing you hold within that guides you to tune in to your body and mind, understand what they're telling you, and do what feels healthy to release and settle your hurt. It's what helps you to recognize that you're experiencing belonging and to create more of these moments.

Your core wisdom pushes you to clock and name sensations inside your body—like if there's a buzzing in your upper chest, a tingling at the back of your neck, a throbbing in your jawline, a burning between your left foot and knee, or numbness throughout your body. In building your core wisdom, you become more and more comfortable using words like warmth, expansion, chills, fuzziness, heaviness, heat, and tightness, to describe what you're sensing. And you're able to identify the feelings coming up within you, like being centered, grateful, excited, hopeful, or tender; angry, disconnected, frustrated, heartbroken, or sad; and bored, fragile, scared, or worried.

Your core wisdom enables you to let go of energy and negativity you're holding by automatically calming your body through movements that help to discharge stress—like trembling, twitching, shaking, and crying. It empowers you to become more aware of the connection between your body and the environment you're in, including how you're reacting to the people and the stimuli that are around you.

In growing your core wisdom, you'll notice beautiful changes in your body—like your back is less tense, the knots in your neck are lessening, your digestive issues are slowing down, your sleep is more restful, you're taking deeper breaths, and you're feeling joy and lightness inside you. You'll pause more often in moments when you're feeling belonging to soak in the warmth. You'll find when sensations come up, you're less likely to override them. For example, when you feel the weight of tears starting to form in your eyes, you'll just start to cry instead of holding back. You may even hear The Voice say *Don't cry*. But you'll just go ahead and do it anyway or you may say something back like, "I've got this," and then let your body release whatever comes up—which, in the end, will feel so good because you've released energy that wanted to leave you.

> " Core wisdom is the knowing you hold within that guides you to tune in to your body and mind, understand what they're telling you, and do what feels healthy to release and settle your hurt.

When it comes to your mind, your core wisdom can help you to pause more and quiet your internal noise, so that you're better able to catch the mean things you say to *yourself* about *yourself*. It can drive you to rewire your brain by replacing harmful messages with more positive and loving beliefs about who you are and your greatness. It can lead you to interrupt the looping in your mind about negative experiences. And it can encourage you to abandon your Performing Self mask and PPA armor so you live more authentically.

In cultivating core wisdom, you'll notice amazing changes in your mind as well—like you're uncovering more of your negative self-talk. And you're more focused on unlearning and rebuilding the messaging that swirls in your head. And maybe you'll clock that you're using more of a growth mindset. Or you're now anchored to the belief you can heal, thrive, and soar. Or you feel safer to be who you really are. And when all of this happens, you'll notice your mind is filled with loving thoughts about how beautiful it feels to belong.

Between your body and your mind, you can use your core wisdom to feel more worthy and whole, be more connected to who you are, become more positive overall, feel more bonded to your beloveds, believe in your self-worth and abilities, showcase your excellence and creativity, and stand in your power—all of which is part of your journey to experience heightened belonging.

In sharing all this with you, I'm highlighting why we want to use our core wisdom as a guide for everything we do. Its healing power and magic can transform any experience we have on our path to belonging.

$$\equiv$$

It's early morning in the winter, and as I pull onto the highway, I'm reminded why some people choose to leave for work at 6 a.m. It's like I have the road to myself, something I'll gladly take since I find most drivers to be profoundly annoying. Working on my road-rage issues is on the "must address" list, but it's moved closer to the bottom given all else I'm unearthing in the intense trauma therapy I've been doing lately. As unsurfaced issues keep coming up, I tell them to "take a number and get in line."

Since there's barely any traffic or snowfall, the drive to the airport will take only twenty-five minutes. This should be enough time for me to perk up and feel alive. I want to be shiny and bright since I haven't seen Santosh for almost a month now. As a musician, this was one of his longer work trips to India, and I've hated being apart this long. People often think of me as a fiercely independent woman, which I am. But this warrior princess loves to snuggle with her man, and, despite what she believed when she was younger, her definition of feminism now has room for both.

The time that Santosh has been away has been a frenzy for me. I've been juggling all kinds of stress. The pandemic is looming—we're a few months away from it fully taking over our lives in this part of the world—but I can already feel the impact on my business. On top of this, we're noticing more and more changes with Mama. As a result, I haven't prioritized my self-care over this last while. I'm feeling a lot like a zombie. I'm numb—I'm not clocking any sensations nor am I pausing to track what's happening in my body. Plus, my mind has become a gigantic playground for noise. I'm sure if I tuned in to what I'm saying to myself, I'd be horrified by the mean self-talk. This is probably one of the reasons I'm not slowing down to go within. I'm in "override" mode, and it's helping me to bulldoze through.

Which is why, as I whip along the highway, I'm starting to notice that I still can't feel anything inside me. No buzzing or butterflies or warmth. No pulses of joy or excitement or anticipation. It may seem like being numb is helpful because I can't feel the intensity of the stress in my life right now. But the problem with being disassociated from my body is that, in a moment that would normally have me all giddy, I'm not sensing any delight inside me either. And this is not how I want to feel as I'm on my way to the airport, nor when I get out of the car and wrap my arms around him.

"Ritu, you know what to do here," I tell myself. I picture a big, sparkly gold treasure chest with the words "Core Wisdom" written on it in gemstones.

But then I hear The Voice say, *No, it's too much work.*

I sigh. Not this back and forth again.

Before this mental ping-ponging gets out of hand, I turn on some kirtan music. Its heavy drumming rhythm is my go-to for signaling to my body and mind that I'm about to dig into my core wisdom. As the calming sounds and vibrations fill the car, I reach over to my purse, which is perched on the front passenger seat. I shove my right hand into the side pocket and pull out my lavender mist, which I often use to help me with breathwork. Squirting a few pumps into both my face and around me, I start taking slow breaths in through my nose, pushing the air deep down into the bottom of my lungs. As my diaphragm contracts and moves down, my belly pushes out. I remind myself to focus on the exhalations, gently moving the air from my belly, up my chest, and out through my nose. Slower and longer exhales help to bring the body and mind into a state of flow or, put another way, become more settled. And, since I'm finding it hard to feel or sense anything, I need this right now.

A few minutes of this pass, and the only thing I'm clocking now is dryness in my nose from the crackly car air and The Voice's taunting. *See, it's not working.*

"I've got this," I calmly respond. I'm mindful that it may take a few different practices to help me.

I dig back into my sparkly gold treasure chest and decide to pull out the body awareness practice I use when I'm having trouble falling asleep or feeling anything inside me: I do a body scan. By this I mean that I slowly and deliberately bring my attention to different parts of my body to check in on what I'm sensing in that area, see if any related emotions are coming up, and figure out if I need to move or adjust my body.

Today, I start my body scan with my toes, where I pause and literally ask myself, "What are you noticing in your toes right now?" as I pay attention for tingling, twitching, or anything to come up, along with any feelings of sadness, excitement, or whatever else might surface.

As I continue with my drive, I make my way bit by bit up across my body to the crown of my head, all while breathing deeply and taking in the lavender-scented air. By the time I get to the top of my head, there's a light buzz pulsing from my feet to my upper thighs. I put my right hand onto my chest between my breasts and feel the kirtan's rhythm beating deeply there. I'm now literally holding my heart in my hand. It all feels so soothing.

"I'm safe," I say to myself. "I'm good. Everything is good."

A wave of gratitude and love washes over me. I exhale forcefully.

Yes, everything is good. Because I've got my core wisdom treasure chest that's filled with practices I've picked up along my healing journey, not to mention some of them are already in my blood, thanks to my incredible ancestors. I now know I can use my core wisdom to help me with anything. Including this moment.

Time has flown by and I'm now at the airport. I catch a glimpse of a drum case on a trolley. As it moves toward me, I know it's him. I run up and tackle him with a huge hug and a zillion kisses. Then I bury my face into his neck to breathe in his smell.

Squeezing him even harder, I gush, "I *really* missed you."

And, as I share this, I feel it throughout my body.

YOUR TREASURE CHEST OF CORE WISDOM PRACTICES

When I was in my twenties and early thirties, if you'd asked me if I understood the magic of core wisdom, without skipping a beat I would have blurted out something like, "Well, of course I do." But I now know I was barely scratching the surface. From my Performing Self mask and my PPA armor to my body tension, back pain, gut health, sleep patterns, anxiety levels, negative self-talk, and energetic flow, I didn't get the full extent of it.

Even during my early years of doing yoga and mindfulness, I still wasn't focusing on using my core wisdom to tell me what I needed or wanted. For example, when I walked into a room or I met someone for the first time, I might have heard things in my head like "I don't trust this person" or "this doesn't feel right," but I'd often push those thoughts down because I thought I was being overcritical. It wasn't until I started to constantly track and name sensations and feelings in my body—like noticing a tightness in my chest instead of a warm tingling while chatting with someone I didn't know well—that my core wisdom truly kicked in.

And now that it has, it's rocked my world.

Given how powerful core wisdom is, you may be wondering how you can grow more of it. Here's the secret to making this happen: We develop our core wisdom by using healing practices like the ancient and ancestral traditions I named in the last chapter combined with the body- and mind-based strategies I've been sharing in this chapter. Specifically, I'm talking about adding strategies like the ones in this list to your healing treasure chest:

- **Breathwork techniques** like belly breathing, Kapalabhati, Nadi Shodhana, and anything else that prompts you to be more intentional about how you're breathing, so that you can calm and regulate your body and mind
- **Movement-focused rituals** like yoga, tai chi, qigong, capoeira, dancing (especially when it's to drums), and anything else that moves your body in such a way that you're combining breathwork with discharging emotions and energy to settle your system
- **Vibration-based experiences** like chanting, ululating, singing, toning, humming, and anything else that causes a pulsation inside you to help stir up and let go of sensations and emotions
- **Touch-centric activities** like massage, acupuncture, cuddling with your beloveds, using heat, and anything else that releases tension, is soothing, and signals to your body that it's safe and supported
- **Body-awareness routines** like the breathwork, movement-focused, vibration-based, and touch-centric practices I mentioned above, but

also body scans and anything else that helps you to sense and name what
you're holding inside you

- **Mindfulness moments** like meditating, journaling, therapy, self-reflection
exercises, talk circles, taking a pause, and anything else that quiets the
noise in your mind so that you can feel more present, interrupt negative
narratives, manage your thoughts, clock when belonging is happening,
and rewire your brain

- **Holistic health habits** like eating tons of veggies, avoiding sugar, drinking
truckloads of water, minimizing intoxicants, getting lots of sleep, exer-
cising regularly, making love, having fun, and anything else that brings
you into balance

In looking at this list, I'm struck by how healing practices and core wisdom
go hand in hand. The more we leverage healing practices, the more we grow our
core wisdom. And the more we grow our core wisdom, the more we're drawn
to using healing practices.

It's a beautiful cycle of soul work that reminds us about what we need and
what's best for us. The chemistry between our healing practices and core
wisdom pushes us to focus on belly breathing. It inspires us to use movement
to release energy but knows there's a difference between using our body for
activity and going within to settle ourselves. It leads us to dance to drumming
rhythms like no one is watching. It guides us to hum, chant, sing, and ululate
loudly. It steers us to be in nature with trees, plants, mountains, water, and
animals. It moves us to color, paint, draw, sculpt, sing, dance, drum, write,
and knit. It encourages us to work with a therapist or body worker when we
need an expert to help us.

> " Healing practices and core wisdom go hand in hand.
> The more we leverage healing practices, the more we
> grow our core wisdom. And the more we grow our
> core wisdom, the more we're drawn to using healing
> practices.

All of these practices become part of our rewarding work to heal along the beautiful and hard path to experiencing belonging. Our core wisdom knows that we need a mix of practices to heal—that one approach alone for the rest of our lives won't be enough and, since many of them are connected, we're more likely to have a greater impact on our healing experiences when we use several of them. It also knows that healing is a marathon, not a sprint. But wherever we start, it doesn't need to be perfect; it just needs to be our best in the moment. As we heal and grow, we may realize that our old best isn't enough anymore. When that happens, we move the dial. We keep ramping up and moving on.

≡

I'm lying face down on a massage table, which is one of my favorite places to be. The sound of ocean waves coming out of the speakers, the bergamot scent wafting through the air, the heating pad on the table, and the deep release I'll feel shortly in my body, I'm here for it all.

My wizard of a massage therapist has just started to take me through his regular list of questions: Are the lights dim enough? Is the pillow under your feet in the right place? Is the face cradle the right height? Back in the day, I would automatically respond "yes" to anything I was asked. But now, I pause after each query to tune in to see if my body is telling me the lighting feels right, my feet are good, and my face is not smooshed. I'm getting used to scanning my body and mind for what they're telling me, regardless of what I'm doing.

I share with him that I'd love for the heating pad to be turned up a bit. I'm all about using warmth to feel good. Heating devices, including Papa Bhasin's homemade bean bags, are littered around my home for the same reason. The heat feels so nice and immediately brings me into my body.

I hear a clicking noise and then he asks if I'm ready to start. "Yup," I murmur through the opening of the cradle. Gently pulling the sheet down to my tailbone, he instructs me to take three deep breaths in and out, all through my nose. I'm reminded that even here on the massage table at the spa, breathwork is wondrous. I can hear Swami Ji's voice in my head from one of our pranayama lessons at the ashram, reminding us that, of course, without breath, there is no life. And, since we're already doing it, we might as well learn how to do it more mindfully, which means moving away from taking short, shallow breaths.

I fill my lungs deeply with air, as I'm now quite accustomed to doing. And with that, his strong hands start to make their way up and down my back.

As my massage therapist continues with his magic, I feel myself melt into the table. Massage is one of the healing practices my parents pushed me to use from when I was very young. They even gifted me my first handheld body massager sometime in the nineties. I affectionately named it E.T. because of how much it looked like the main character from the 1980s sci-fi film. Little did I know that E.T. would eventually be joined by a full array of friends for my feet, neck, arms, legs, back, and face. Or that this was the starting point of a lifelong commitment to using massage as part of my healing and self-care—to let go of not only tension, but grief and hurt as well.

I start thinking of the eye-opening moment in my twenties when I first realized massages help to release clusters of sorrow that build up inside us and not just knots and kinks. I was going through a bad breakup and, in fine PPA fashion, I threw myself into working really long hours almost every day. If I could keep achieving, maybe it would distract me from the anguish of my broken heart. Without even knowing it, I had stopped seeing my friends and family as much, and I was basically isolating myself to cope.

It had been ages since I'd had a massage, given my tight spending budget at the time, but I decided to save up to see a massage therapist a friend had recommended. As I lay on the table and she worked on my body, I was being jumpy and jittery. About ten minutes into the treatment, she asked very softly, "Ritu, how are you feeling?"

Like an automaton, I immediately replied, "Good!"

Leaning over ever so slightly, she tenderly half-whispered into my ear, "The body needs to be touched, and your body needs this." And with those words, I came undone. For our remaining time together, I flowed between weeping and full-on sobbing.

I didn't know the importance of this then, but I sure do now: as one of the most social creatures out there, humans crave healthy touch. The moment we see a friend or baby cry, we automatically want to reach over to embrace them, because touch can be reassuring and healing. It can help us to release the hurt we're holding and to feel safe, settled, and loved. And this is why my body needed touch in that moment.

"Okay, Ritu, we're done now," my wizard therapist says to me. The sixty minutes have flown by. Like being in Shavasana, I feel so free and relaxed. I wish I could feel like this in every moment. Of course, I recognize that's unrealistic, but I also know that, as I continue to do my healing work, I'll have so many more moments like this.

TAKE A MOMENT TO REFLECT

Prior to reading this chapter, to what extent were you aware of your core wisdom? How have you been using it until now? What gifts has it given you? How has it impacted your sense of belonging?

When you're experiencing belonging, what does it feel like in your body? What sensations and feelings come up inside you? What thoughts go through your mind?

Which healing practices have you gravitated to in the past? How have these healing practices helped you to grow your core wisdom? What else are you doing to develop your core wisdom?

Going forward, which healing practices will you add to your treasure chest to expand your core wisdom? How will you integrate these practices into your life? How will these practices help you on your journey to belong?

What challenges are in your way to developing your core wisdom? What can you do to address those challenges?

Questions for You to Explore Across All Chapters:

What are the key insights you've picked up from reading this chapter?

Which stories or messages most resonated with you? Why?

What are one or two things you'll do differently going forward?

CHAPTER NINE

WE HEAL FOR OURSELVES AND FOR OTHERS

"You know, I often feel invisible in our circle, like I don't matter."

My words come out so softly it's almost a whisper. My sister and two girlfriends stare at me wide eyed. It suddenly becomes so quiet in the hotel room that I can hear my own breathing. I look down and continue, "It's like there are tiers in our friend group, and I'm on the outer ring. Sometimes it's like I'm nonexistent." I'm struggling to make eye contact with them as I share what I've been holding inside me for some time now.

I quickly glance up. They look surprised. They weren't expecting me to say any of this. And frankly, neither was I. Not in this moment when we're away on a girls' trip. I can't believe these words are finally pouring out of my mouth. And I'm doing it so bluntly. My heart is pounding and my cheeks are burning. I'm almost starting to tremble—the fear and shame, coupled with the exhilaration of getting this out of me, are overwhelming.

But now that I've taken the lid off, I can't stop: "Sometimes when we're hanging out, I'll notice that I ask about something, but you just respond to each other. Like, none of you will look at me when you're talking. It's like I'm not there. Even though *I'm* the one who asked the question in the first place.

"Or when I message in our WhatsApp group, there are many times when no one acknowledges what I've said. It's like crickets chirping." The feelings are now overflowing. "But when one of you messages, it's like ping, ping, ping..." My voice trails off as I start to tear up.

There's a moment of awkward silence, which is then filled with a burst of "oh wows" and "aww" sounds and assurances.

I feel both sheepish and grateful.

I'm ashamed because I can't believe that in my forties—even in the midst of writing this book—it still feels like I'm accepting crumbs in my relationships. Because my feelings of unworthiness lead me to sometimes take less than I deserve. And in spite of all I've learned, it's hard for me to call these moments out for fear that love will be taken away. It's like how I felt back when I was a kid, hiding behind the portable classrooms recess after recess instead of telling my teachers or my parents about the rejection I was experiencing. Or in other moments when I've felt like a yo-yo.

But, at the same time, I'm thankful for the work I've done to get me to a point where I'm able to address this pattern of behavior. Lately my sessions with my trauma therapist have been devoted to exploring how my childhood feelings of unworthiness show up for me now as an adult, including how they still drive me to be my Performing Self. Because of our work together, I finally understand the niggling feeling I've been having about my friend group, which has led to a huge insight: my childhood trauma is leading me to feel like I don't belong in our friend circle, *and* I'm afraid to share this with them in fear they won't play with me anymore.

In my therapy work, we also talk about how, in my thirties, after coming back from the ashram, I broke up with my dysfunctional friend crew even though I worried I'd be friendless and lonely. Instead of having to hang out with my parents on Friday and Saturday nights for the rest of time, it made space for me to invite new friendships into my life where I felt much safer to be me. So I know I'll be fine if I speak my truth now.

And I *am* fine when I do—not just because I've stood in my power but because my friend group receives my vulnerability exactly as I hoped they would. They're open, kind, and supportive.

As the energy in the room settles a bit, one of my girlfriends asks if she can share something with me. I nod my head emphatically. She tells me she sometimes feels like I seem uninterested in the group chatter and too busy with work to engage. The others chime in with agreement. As I take in what they're sharing, I get why they feel this way. It's true, I do deliberately linger on the outskirts with them. Some of this is because I feel they don't like me as much as they do each other, so I'm scared to engage more.

But when I dig deeper in reflecting on this, I see that, at times, I'm also only giving out crumbs in my friendships and I too can treat others like a yo-yo—both of which also connect back to my woundedness. My friends and sister also have a longing to belong. They too are looking for people around whom they feel safe to be authentic and vulnerable, and who'll accept and embrace them for who they are. By healing my pain, I'll be able to better cultivate this type of energy with them.

It's a huge "aha" moment for me. And there are more to come.

> " Our relationships become mirrors of the healing work
> we still need to do.

Over time, I offer more feedback to them, and they do the same with me. One of them tells me I can be judgmental and elitist, and my Bhenji spirit can be off-putting. While I've received these comments in other relationships before, and I know all this to be true, it's still hard for me to hear. But my heart is open and accepting of what's being revealed to me, because bettering how I treat others is a key part of my healing. It's not just about how people treat me.

So, going forward with my friend group, I pay more attention to what I'm saying, how I'm saying it, and whether I need to be saying it at all. And I anchor to being more embodied when I'm with them, because when my system is activated because of stress, I can go into judgment and Bhenji overload.

Not only do these moments highlight for me the role I play in creating belonging for myself and for others, they're also pivotal in affirming my commitment to continuing to heal my childhood trauma. In the end, I know I'll be better for it.

≡

When we carry feelings of being unworthy and unlovable, our pain will keep showing up in our lives—especially if we're not doing our healing work. The wounds we carry will have a profound impact on how we treat ourselves, how we treat others, and how we let others treat us. All this connects with a powerful take-away: our relationships become mirrors of the healing work we still need to do.

In fact, relationships give rise to important experiences with others that are not only essential for healing but are everything for unlocking belonging. It's along the path of bonding with ourselves and with others that we watch the seeds of healing slowly fill our garden with flowers. And, because of this, we must keep planting.

> This chapter uncovers why your healing journey must focus on creating belonging experiences for yourself *and* for others.

WHAT YOUR RELATIONSHIP MIRRORS REVEAL

Given how significant your personal connections are for creating belonging and joy in your life, you'll want to dig deep into understanding what's happening in your relationships and what the mirrors are telling you.

With friends, you'll hopefully cling to a cluster of people around whom you feel free to exhale and just be. But it may not feel like it's enough, especially if you haven't made real friends with yourself yet and if you're still looking outward to fill your cup. If that's the case, you'll likely also gravitate to those who just crack open the door of acceptance, but, when you're with them, you desperately need to mask and armor. You know you're constantly being evaluated, but you hold the mistaken belief that this is better than being lonely.

With family, you might struggle with creating boundaries to protect you from how you're being treated. Because of deeply entrenched childhood dynamics, you may continue to be on the receiving end of toxic, abusive, and judgmental behavior, and your fear of being punished or abandoned may often hold you back from standing in your power. It'll feel difficult to draw the lines you don't want them to cross—for example, in how they speak to you, what they're entitled to comment on, when they can spend time with you, and much more. And this is why you may keep eating the hurt that comes your way.

With lovers, you might keep choosing badly since you continue to feel unlovable and flawed. You're likely to overstay in relationships with people who hurt you while you hurt them back. It can be a destructive, ongoing cycle. Plus, because you feel lost and unhappy about who you are, the checklist you create for who you're meant to be with is so far off from what you really need. And, of course, this leads to heartbreak and then more heartbreak.

> " It's lonelier to be surrounded by people who don't accept us for who we are than to stand on our own.

With work colleagues, it might feel as though you're putting on a big Broadway production for them, one where you're on stage with your mask and armor to help you move up the professional ladder. And the confusing thing is the curated image you're putting out there does help. On the surface, it may look like you're winning, and, in some respects, you are. Except that the price tag is high: you have to deal with endless workplace gaslighting, and you constantly feel soulless.

You may even engage in these self-sabotaging types of behavior with random people out in the world—we're not immune in our interactions with strangers.

These experiences reinforce why our core wisdom is crucial. It helps us to see the cracks in our connections with others and do the work to mend them to build stronger bonds. Over time, as we do our healing work and use our core wisdom, we'll come to see that it's lonelier to be surrounded by people who don't accept us for who we are than to stand on our own. We'll learn that committing to a life of authenticity will transform who and how we love, and, given this, we'll shed all kinds of toxic relationships from our life. We'll draw boundaries and make better choices about who gets to be around us. And, in doing so, we'll give off all kinds of radiant energy that helps us to attract and be encased by gems, around whom we experience sweet belonging.

All of this will happen because we've committed to doing our healing work. And when it does, it'll feel beautiful.

≡

I hear Santosh's deep baritone laugh from across the room at the party, and I immediately look over in his direction. He's standing with a few buddies, and they're all howling. I'm sure he's in the middle of cracking jokes. He's so funny. I'm just glad that others also get to enjoy his hysterical energy.

Now that he's grabbed my attention, I keep staring at him in admiration. His eyes and teeth both sparkle against his shiny dark-brown skin. I love to watch him when he's not looking. He's so beautiful. But it's more than that. In taking him in, I'm getting swept up in waves of gratitude. "I can't believe I found you," I think to myself.

He's so different from who I thought I'd choose to be my life partner. In my early twenties, for a man to get through the door with me, he had to be "handsome, smart, and kind." These were table stakes, and the bar was high. I vigilantly assessed for these attributes, and I wouldn't budge. But I also added on a five-star ranking system for assessing boyfriend candidates. The more stars, the greater the likelihood we'd date. "A feminist" and "a good cook" others agreed on. But "likes hip hop," "is a good dancer," and "dresses well" raised eyebrows, including with Mama Bhasin, who shot me a disturbed look when I first told her.

Back then, while the clock had started to tick on finding a suitable husband, preferably Indian as per my parents, I had lots of runway because I was still young and just starting my career. It was fine for me to run social experiments in my dating life for a bit before I turned to getting married and having kids.

The moment I hit thirty, everything changed. At every turn, from my Punjabi elders to my girlfriends to work colleagues to societal messages, I felt bulldozing, misogynistic pressure to get hitched and spawn. But I was nowhere near being able to make this happen. I was carrying around a massive sack of childhood trauma filled with pain related to not knowing who I was. And there were a few other things going on too: I was still struggling with my cultural identities; I was rejecting men who weren't White corporate types; and I was using my career as a shield to protect me from the coercion to settle down.

Almost every decision I made back then about who to let into my life ended up hurting badly. From experiencing emotional angst to relentless infidelity to settling for boyfriends who weren't good for me, I had my heart broken so many times. It was like I moved into the Heartbreak Hotel and didn't think I deserved to leave. And the overpowering messaging to just pick someone and get on with it made it a thousand times worse.

The shame I felt about constantly being alone, then heartbroken, then alone, then heartbroken, then alone, then heartbroken was unbearable at times. Especially as it related to my love life, I felt so lost, broken, flawed, and ashamed.

What saved me in the end was my core wisdom. Through the deep healing work I doubled down on, especially in my late thirties, I finally started to pull off my Performing Self mask, revealing both to myself and to the world, this is who I really am. And given that this is who I really am, this is what I need and want in a partner.

And this is why my heart chose him, in particular: a professional musician who's repelled by things that scream "corporate" or reflect the establishment, who's every bit mellow to my incredible intensity, who's down with smashing gender norms including not having kids and having me in the driver's seat, who's sweet and soft by nature, and around whom my body feels at ease, calm, and settled. And of course, he has all five stars.

I'm still staring at him when he glances over in my direction. Our eyes lock, and we smile at each other. He turns his head a bit away from his friends and blows me a few air kisses. I giggle and do the same back. My girlfriend catches this all go down and shrieks, "Oh my god, you two are so cute!"

I immediately turn to her and say, "Thanks, but don't let that fool you. We fought the whole way over here." As I launch into my list of grievances, our conversation turns to how hard romantic relationships are.

I will never shy away from saying that I find it so hard to consistently show up as an intentional, empathetic, and compassionate partner. My childhood trauma and demons from previous dating experiences constantly show up in the mirror that's held up for me in our dynamic. I'm still learning how to fight and communicate better, and both take a lot of effort. I even worry that our relationship will implode one day, and that I'll end up alone back in the Heartbreak Hotel, which I know is a possibility.

But I also feel deep to my core that the safe space we've created in our relationship is moving me to take care of my wounds. Our love is helping me to heal. I already feel more whole and at peace because of our union. This is what I always wanted and what I was looking for.

And this is what belonging feels like.

HOW YOU TREAT OTHERS MATTERS

In study after study about what brings us happiness in life, the quality of our relationships consistently lands at the top of the list. We need healthy, deep, and meaningful ties with loving people to feel safe and joyful throughout our years on this planet—this is what our innate need to experience belonging is all about. Not only do these types of bonds give us a place to do the self-work that's needed to keep healing and growing, but they offer us refuge to exhale and belong.

I call these types of loving connections "cloud relationships." I picture a big, fluffy, soft cloud that I can fall into when I'm feeling down or hurt or exhausted from the hard stuff that's coming my way. The same thing comes to mind when I think of all the people in my life who I can rely on to lift me up during tough times and to share moments of lightness and laughter. They're my clouds.

We must have cloud relationships to get the love, safety, comfort, and thrills we need along this emotional roller coaster ride called life. Our circle of clouds can include anyone who helps us to feel good: lovers, friends, family, workmates, classmates, leaders, mentors, and anybody else who holds us up when we need it. In their midst, we can speak our mind, let out our ugliest cries, share our darkest insecurities, sit in stillness, laugh like a banshee, and have exhilarating fun. It's in their presence that our body will signal we're feeling belonging.

" We need healthy, deep, and meaningful ties with loving people to feel safe and joyful throughout our years on this planet—this is what our innate need to experience belonging is all about.

But you also want to show up as clouds for your beloveds—because they're looking for clouds, too, and how you treat others matters. Serving as a cloud is also what belonging is about. You want to offer your beloveds healthy and unconditional love, empathy, and good times since they're on healing journeys too. They need love and support just as you do. You can be there for them by tuning in to their needs, honoring what they share with you, ensuring they belong based on who they are and not who you want them to be, showering them with your affection and respect, and having a truckload of laughs with them.

Ultimately, cloud relationships are uplifting and healing for everyone, not to mention they help to create communities and cultures that are rooted in authenticity and belonging.

But as we keep healing, we don't just show up for our clouds. Because we're committed to goodness, we know that every one of our actions, thoughts, emotions, and comments can have a domino effect on those around us. As I'll talk about in *Belonging*, we become even more intentional with our choices because we want to cultivate experiences of belonging for everyone around us—even complete strangers.

To make this happen, we bring our empowered energy into all our interactions. We start to do things we may have held back from doing in the past. We speak. We act. We say no. We say yes. We ask why. We have difficult conversations. We shut down lies. We drop the haters. We flock to people who are about kindness. We step forward. We step aside. We listen more. We call out bad behavior. We post, follow, like, and share carefully. We read, watch, listen, and consume wisely. We pay attention to the language we use. And we do this all—and more—because we know our spirit impacts others' experiences with belonging.

Even when it feels exhausting and relentless to be intentional and meticulous with how we act, we keep at it.

We keep trying.

We don't give up.

Because we know there's an interconnectedness of being, especially when it comes to belonging. We need each other. So, let's be there for each other.

=

My cheeks hurt as the snow whips against my face. "Of all the days to choose to take the bus!" I mutter to myself as I stand at the street corner. I'm on my way to lunch with a client near the business district and, to get there, I'm braving Toronto's transit system on a cold winter day.

It's just me at the stop along with an elderly man who looks East Asian and is using a cane. When the bus finally pulls up, I wait for him to get on first. It's fairly crowded, and so we both shuffle into the tight clearing at the front. The bus jerks as it continues on, and, in unison, we quickly grab onto the same pole. I feel Ritu Putri energy start to pulse in my body. Every muscle inside me is on high alert watching this elderly man who's now precariously teetering between the pole and his cane.

My eyes dart to the priority seating row right in front of us to see if there's a seat available. Not one is empty. My detective radar turns on as I start to scan the taken seats. I know from my inclusion work that we don't want to make assumptions about who should or shouldn't be sitting in these seats. But I also know that many people who don't need priority seating will often sit here. And in this moment, I'm suspicious.

I'm now glaring at the mix of people, none of whom are moving or offering the elderly man their seat. No one is flinching even a bit. They're doing what people often do in awkward moments when they know they should give up something they don't want to: they've fixed their eyes intensely on an inanimate object in hopes that no one will look at or speak to them.

I begin to banter with myself in my head. It starts off with, "Should I say something to these sitter-downers?" to which I immediately shoot back a "Yes!" But then it turns into a debate. As an inclusion expert, I find myself in a rapid game of mental ping-pong where I'm playing both sides. On one side of the table, I'm pointing out to myself that I shouldn't overstep by sweeping in as a savior based on what I think people need. But the comeback from the other side is compelling: it's crucial I take action against what feels unjust and disrespectful, especially given how I feel about belonging—and in this moment, I worry that this elderly man isn't being seen or respected.

The back-and-forth carries on for about half a stop when the following image pops into my head: Mama Bhasin wobbling between a cane and a pole while nary a person offers her a seat. I feel the Putri energy take over my entire being. I stop deliberating and instead surrender to my core wisdom. Even if I have this wrong, it'll be a learning moment and I'll grow from it.

"Excuse me," I suddenly blurt out to the elderly man. "Would you like to sit down?" Which seat I'm going to offer him, I have no idea.

"No, no, thank you," he responds.

Since I've been trained by Punjabi immigrant parents to decline all acts of kindness at least eight times before finally saying yes, I know to not stop at his first refusal.

So, I ask him once again. And he nicely repeats a no.

But I still feel the agitation inside me, and I just can't bring myself to leave it there. In a flash, I look at the sitter-downers and loudly pronounce: "If you'd wanted to sit down, I would've asked one of these people to give up their seat." Then I bring my gaze back to him.

He smiles. I smile. A White woman standing near us smiles. And she also says, "Good for you. I wanted to say something too." I nod my head at her both to acknowledge what she's said and to signal "Yes, you could have." But I'll tell you who doesn't smile: the sitter-downers. A few of them are now scowling in my direction. Thankfully I only have a few stops to go, and I decide that it's my turn to stare at an inanimate object.

As I get off the bus and trudge through the snow toward the restaurant, I reflect on how taken aback I am that I used my voice so assertively. Not only was the Ritu of years past unable to speak up for herself in moments where her belonging was being hurt, she also struggled to call out disrespectful behavior directed at others. Yes, I might have felt the fury in my body, but I absolutely wouldn't have been able to open my mouth to speak out to random strangers in public. Especially if I thought I'd be overstepping.

But the seeds of healing have now been planted. What's important to me is that I live my truth, while recognizing my connection to all other beings. I'm starting to deeply appreciate that, in any given moment, I get to choose how I treat myself *and* how I treat others. It's a valuable takeaway: in any interaction, we help to create or tear down belonging for others in whether we choose to speak, what we choose to say, and how we choose to act. In some moments, it'll feel safe to be visible and vocal, while in others it won't. Sometimes we might freeze in the moment or not act, out of fear of being judged, or decide we just don't want to.

And all of this is fine.

Because this is what it looks like to be on the winding path to unlocking the beauty of belonging.

TAKE A MOMENT TO REFLECT

If relationships are a mirror of the healing we need to do, what thoughts do you have about the self-work you'd like to do going forward?

Who are your clouds and why? What does belonging feel like in their presence? What are you doing to cultivate these relationships?

Who are you a cloud for? What do you do to show up for them? How does it feel to know they experience belonging in your midst? Where does this show up in your body?

In wanting to create belonging for others, how will you change some of your behaviors going forward?

Questions for You to Explore Across All Chapters:

What are the key insights you've picked up from reading this chapter?

Which stories or messages most resonated with you? Why?

What are one or two things you'll do differently going forward?

BELONGING

CHAPTER TEN

BELONGING AND AUTHENTICITY GO HAND IN HAND

t's been almost ten years since David first reached out to me. As one of the few students of color at his law school, he was looking for help on how to navigate being a lonely-only in an already tough environment. I could relate. I can remember sitting by myself, with my mask and armor on, in the library a few weeks into law school at a mahogany-like wood table that screamed "designed by colonizer." As I sat there flipping through my student directory, I counted the number of people who looked like me. I knew my data-collection methodology was flawed, but the outcome affirmed "Here's why you don't belong."

David and I hit it off right away. After chatting a few times, we came up with an idea: he'd pull together a group of five first-year law students from backgrounds like ours, and we'd create a mentorship circle of sorts. The plan was to meet up regularly, so I could offer up wisdom on how to get ahead in a world that's filled with bumps, especially for people like us. I would get to be Ritu Bhenji in all her glory. This is how the six of us came together.

It's heartwarming how quickly we all bonded, given how different we are. We span a range of identities: African, Caribbean, South Asian, and Canadian; Black, Brown, and multi-racial; Sikh, Hindu, and Christian; women and men (all of us cis); queer and hetero; and there's a ten- to fifteen-year age gap between us.

But despite our differences, we've been tied together for more than a decade by authenticity, resonance, trust, and love, and I no longer pulsate Bhenji energy with them—I'm just one of them. We connect because we all know how hard it is to navigate a world where we stick out, experience hurtful things, struggle to be who we are, and feel torn between cultures. We bond over our craving to live our best by being our true selves. We want to shine in life and, in doing so, make our elders proud. This is why I named our group the "Sparks Circle"—because I can feel the flame of passion, brilliance, and potential burning within each of us.

Tonight, we're sitting around my kitchen counter munching on the food I've put out for us. We're swapping stories about how we're both deeply grateful to our respective immigrant parents *and* frustrated that they still don't understand who we really are. We just finished chatting about how, elitism aside, we can't wrap our minds around why White men love golf so much. Next up, we'll dig into how to keep looking hot as we age. Later in the evening, we'll get into society's hateful systems and the types of people one should never marry.

"Ritu, I'm going to open up this bottle," Winston says to me as he points to the lovely bottle of red wine he brought. I nod enthusiastically.

Each time our circle gets together, whether it's at a restaurant, on a video call, or at my kitchen counter, we take turns giving each other a candid, uncensored update on every aspect of our lives. Plus, we always openly talk about what we're having a hard time with, whatever that may be. Every one of us does this, every time.

"Is it my turn?" I ask. It's confirmed. Brian just wrapped up, and I'm next.

"Tell us everything!" Vidushi exclaims, her eyes sparkling as they always do.

I don't hesitate for even a second before sharing how hard a time I'm having in life right now—from struggling to write this book to managing my business during the pandemic to experiencing diminished mental health, it's been rough. But it's when I start talking about my heartache from elder care that I start to fully break down. As I share, my voice cracks and the tears flow, especially when I mention that Mama Bhasin will likely only be here in spirit by the time this book comes out.

They know exactly what I need in this moment as I vulnerably reveal my angst: they lean in both physically and spiritually, and they give me reassuring words that signal they're there to hold me up. I sense their love and acceptance for who I am. Warmth flows throughout my body as I exhale and just be.

After taking a few breaths, I tell them my newest concern: that because Santosh and I probably won't have children, I'm worried about who is going to look after me when I'm old. I then declare, in fine Ritu Bhenji fashion, "You guys have to take care of me." My command doesn't go as expected. Rather than crying out "For sure!" in unison, there are a few awkward "umms," and "ahhhs," while most eyes stare down at the food platters.

"Oh my god, really?!" I cry out.

They immediately start debating among themselves. They strategically decide that the youngest person in our group, who couldn't make it this evening, will be my primary caregiver. I agree to this and commit to informing him of this great news. We share a laugh, and the conversation moves on.

As I start to clear the plates, they continue to chat away, and I remark to myself that I just adore spending time with them. I love that we've created a safe space where we can openly talk about the wild and unpredictable ups and downs of life, while encouraging each other to keep at it—and have lots of fun together while doing this. But what I value most is that we embrace each other's authenticity, we celebrate our respective wins, and we affirm the greatness that lives in all of us.

This is what belonging is about.

≡

Belonging is the feeling of being accepted for who you are by your own self and by the people you choose to be bonded with, so that you feel seen and valued. It's about your instinctive need to reveal your authenticity and, in doing so, knowing you'll be honored and respected for who you are across your identities. Because belonging is a feeling, your body will signal to you that you're experiencing acceptance through the comforting and affirming sensations within you. You'll feel safe, calm, and at ease.

Authenticity is the practice of consistently choosing to know, embrace, and be who you are, especially what makes you different and unique, as much as possible. It's at the root of what I call the Authenticity Principle: the life tenet that when you consistently choose to be authentic, you'll feel more joyful and connected to yourself, you'll bring this spirit into your interactions, and in doing so you'll invite people to do the same back with you. When you're practicing authenticity, you'll feel warm and uplifting sensations all over your body.

Given these definitions, it is easy to see how belonging and authenticity are inextricably intertwined. To experience belonging, you must be able to reveal your authentic self. And when you feel safe to be your authentic self, this is when you experience the greatest belonging.

This connection between belonging and authenticity underscores an essential takeaway: the most important relationship you'll ever cultivate is the one you have with yourself. It's not until you feel seen, accepted, and loved by yourself that you'll enjoy deep and meaningful connection with others. Simply put, you won't experience belonging until you first honor your authentic self.

> This chapter focuses on how you can live more authentically to unlock greater experiences of belonging.

EXPLORING YOUR THREE SELVES

In my book *The Authenticity Principle*, I offer a guide for living more authentically called the Three Selves Framework.

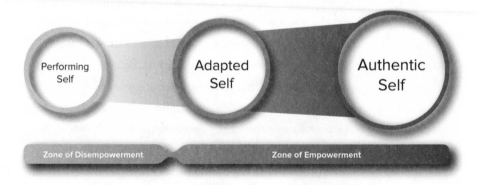

The Performing Self sits on one end of this continuum in the "Zone of Disempowerment," because it hurts your soul to mask and armor up, as we've now explored in *Hurting* and *Healing*. Throughout these pages, as I've been talking about belonging, I've essentially been highlighting the importance of pushing out of your Performing Self and choosing instead to be your Authentic Self or your Adapted Self, both of which are reflections of your authenticity.

To experience the greatest depth of belonging, you want to show up as your Authentic Self as much as possible. Your Authentic Self is who you'd be if there were no negative consequences for how you behave—it's how you'd express your emotions, what body language you'd use, how you'd speak, the words you'd use, how you'd dress, the content you'd share, and so much more. It's the good, the bad, and the ugly of who you are, but because it's the truest reflection of your essence, it feels the best to do. This is why it tops what I call the "Zone of Empowerment."

That said, you can, and sometimes need to, choose to show up as your Adapted Self, especially in moments where being your Authentic Self doesn't feel safe or you just don't want to. Your Adapted Self is who you are when you willingly choose to adjust your behavior from how your Authentic Self would show up because the moment calls for it. For example, I love to cuss like a pirate and, as I already shared, the F-word is one of my favorites, but in this book I'm mentioning frogs instead, in case a child starts to read through the pages. And I'm good with that. Your Adapted Self is happy and willing to make behavioral shifts because it feels fine to do, it serves you, it serves others, and it's still a reflection of your authenticity. It also falls in the "Zone of Empowerment," but when you keep adapting your behavior and it starts to feel like you're conforming or masking, then you're back into the "Zone of Disempowerment."

The reason why I'm digging into the Three Selves Framework in this book is that, as you can see, belonging happens when you choose to show up as your Authentic Self and your Adapted Self. Along your path to belonging, you want to use your core wisdom to help make choices that enable you to be these two Selves—your Authentic Self in particular—instead of living as your Performing Self.

Knowing how and when to flow between your Authentic Self and Adaptive Self is a learned skill. By tuning in to your body and mind, you'll know how you want to behave from minute to minute, person to person, and moment to moment. And the more you rely on your healing practices and core wisdom to make this happen, the greater the likelihood you'll live authentically—which is essential for being accepted and honored for who you are.

> " Belonging and authenticity are inextricably intertwined. To experience belonging, you must be able to reveal your authentic self. And when you feel safe to be your authentic self, this is when you experience the greatest belonging.

=

I'm sitting cross-legged on my couch with my brand-new MacBook in my lap, attempting to create an invoice template in Excel. I just recently completed my MBA and made the bold step of launching my own DEI consulting firm. I now need an invoice template for my new business, in hopes that a client actually hires me. But I'm struggling to build one. It's beyond me how I made it through school without learning how to use this program properly. As a big fan of Word, I don't get why hitting "Enter" takes you to a different cell altogether in Excel and not just to the next line. I want to scream. I wish someone had told me this is how dismal entrepreneurship can be at times.

If it weren't for Stevie Wonder and my time at the ashram, I would never have done the MBA. Nor would I have started my new business. But I made a promise to change how I was living. And I've been doing my best to honor it ever since then.

A few months after the concert, I'm finally honest with myself about my fancy law job: it's killing my spirit. I'm adapting a lot, which is fine, but I'm constantly performing. And it's a rare day I'm showing up as my Authentic Self. I need to quit, but in my mind, I keep hearing the question "If not this, then what?" with no answer to avail. I'm scared about my future, and I don't know what to do.

After several weeks of encouraging myself to share my truth with people I trust, I finally turn to a few of my clouds, because I can be vulnerable and authentic with them. Early one morning, a few months before I head to the ashram, I meet my dear friend Nouman for breakfast to ask for his guidance. Nouman is a business school professor and a fellow DEI professional, and I've known him personally and professionally for years. I respect his wisdom and feel safe to admit my fears to him.

I come running into the restaurant because I'm late to meet him, as usual. As I walk toward the table, I see he's placed a large envelope at my setting. When I pick it up, my eye catches the business school logo in the top right-hand corner, and then I clock that the label is made out to "Ms. Ritu Bhasin." Something about my name being on it matters. My heart flutters. Inside is a letter encouraging me to apply to do an MBA in their year-long executive program, so I can keep working full time while attending classes on weekends. As I settle in, Nouman launches into how doing this exact program changed his life and he knows it'll do the same for me.

I've never thought about doing an MBA before, and my brain isn't having it. For weeks, The Voice gives me all kinds of reasons why I shouldn't take this path: *Since it's an executive program, it'll be filled with real business people, which you're not. How will you juggle both work and school? You can't do both. You're not smart enough to do statistics. It's too expensive. What if you come back from the ashram and decide not to do it? You'll lose your big, fat deposit.* And The Voice also adds this zinger: *Business is evil.*

Nouman keeps on me in the weeks that follow, and, thankfully, he's louder than The Voice. Because he's spot on. The "evil" MBA ends up transforming my life.

So much is revealed as I do the degree. Not only am I adept at understanding complex business concepts, I'm smarter than many of the "legit" business types in my class. They talk a lot, but I also have great value to add. As I coach myself to speak more often, I realize I bought into the messaging that, as a Brown girl born of working-class immigrant parents, I wouldn't be good enough for this program.

I learn that my Authentic Self isn't just a social justice type, I'm an entrepreneurial die-hard too, and I was even born one. I constantly have flashbacks to when I was a daring, adventurous kid, before society's commentary about who I'm supposed to be took over. At fourteen, during the height of my childhood entrepreneurialism, I'd already launched a lawn-mowing business, run a paper route, been a neighborhood magician, and become a children's party entertainer, on top of leading a highly successful babysitting practice.

As I inch closer to finishing the degree, it also becomes clear it's time for me to spread my wings and become the entrepreneur I am in my heart. I want to lead a more authentic life by making my own rules for getting ahead. I want to develop my own way of working, one where I get to be my Authentic Self as much as possible, decide on the work I do, control the messages I put out in the world, and choose who I'm surrounded by. I want to create belonging for myself. And I can do this through the choices I make about how to live, work, and lead.

This is what pushes me to quit my job in the corporate towers to start my own company for which I'm now struggling to create an invoice template. As I work away on the document, I can hear the question "What if no one hires me?!" looping in my head along with visions of going bankrupt and having to move into my parents' basement. But I'm breathing through the anxiousness, using the practices I learned at the ashram. And I'm reminding myself that I finally get to work in a more authentic way.

As I build both my business and my life of belonging, the fire of authenticity that burns inside me will continue to grow. As this keeps unfolding, I'll feel better and better about who I am and the life I'm living. The beauty of belonging will come to encase me.

Not to mention, I'll end up using the invoice template I once created countless times.

CHOOSE TO SHOW UP AS YOUR AUTHENTIC SELF

How do you know you're showing up as your Authentic Self or Adapted Self? How do you know you're experiencing belonging? How do you know you're feeling empowered? Your body will tell you. When you use your core wisdom to tune in to what's happening inside you, the fluttering feelings, sensations, and thoughts will let you know.

Maybe it's a flood of warmth that washes over your chest or a stillness in your belly or a surge of tingles across your back or tears that form in your eyes.

Or maybe you can sense gratitude in your heart. Or joy on your face. Or calmness in your breath.

Or maybe in the thoughts that cross your mind, you can hear yourself say, "This feels so nice" or "I love being around you" or "I don't care what anyone thinks, I'm just going to do me."

And that's not all. You'll know belonging is unfolding in your life because the choices you make will reflect your Authentic Self. In other words, you'll choose to show up in ways that reveal you're honoring yourself, and, in doing so, you signal to others you want them to do the same. For example, you'll choose to:

- Call out the harmful, hurtful, and hateful things that happen to you
- Be at peace with being a mishmash of identities
- Raise your hand for opportunities
- Get people to pronounce your name correctly
- Laugh or cry as loud as you want to
- Practice your faith openly and proudly
- Wear whatever you want
- Adore your body just as it is
- Style your hair however you want to
- Use your native tongue at every opportunity, including in public
- Speak whenever you want to, especially when you're the lonely-only
- Give your opinions even when The Voice tells you not to
- Let go of people who hurt you

Of course, these are just a few of the things you can do to honor and express love for who you are. The important point is, in your journey to belong, you'll want to often pause to reflect on what you're already doing and what more you can choose to make happen. This means choosing to be fiercely authentic, even when you're worried about the negative consequences.

I'll be the first to share with you that I've experienced rejection for being my Authentic Self because my authenticity is "too much" for some. But it's shown me that those who feel that way are not my people since, in their presence, I sense pressure to be my Performing Self. And I don't want to put that mask on. Being more authentic has invited beautiful friendships and experiences into my life, even if the road to get here was bumpy. That's what matters for joy in my life, not caring about the opinions of people who "can't handle" me.

As I continue my journey to live in a fiercely authentic way, I know I still have further to go, but I've made a big dent and this gives me the fuel to keep going. For example, after having my name, Ritu, which means "the four seasons" in Hindi, mispronounced for my whole childhood and all through my twenties, at the age of thirty I finally decided to have every single human say it properly, which is Rih-thu (and my last name is Ba-seen). And while I'm talking about language, I now always use the correct pronunciation when I'm saying South Asian words but speaking in English—e.g., for mantra I'll say mun-thra and not man-tra.

I use my body as a canvas for South Asian culture. I've pierced my nose and donned a hoop ring. I have a tattoo of *Ik Onkar*, the Sikh symbol for One Creator, on my wrist, and scripture from our Japji Sahib prayer down my spine. I wear bright colors, patterns, and styles that scream "Brown and proud." I've grown out my hair into a lion's mane as a visible symbol of being a Sikh, and, even when I do cut it, it's because I want to and not because I feel pressure to. I've shed the desire to be stick thin, and I've embraced the beauty of curves. I've committed to never adding blond highlights to my hair ever again. I bask in the glory of the sun and the dark-brown skin it gives me.

> " It's not until you feel seen, accepted, and loved by yourself that you'll enjoy deep and meaningful connection with others. Simply put, you won't experience belonging until you first honor your authentic self.

And there's more: using many of the healing practices I've told you about, I've worked hard to unlearn the toxic beliefs that led me to only date White men. I embrace my sexuality as a woman, and I'm all about openly talking about it, especially since doing this in all the cultures I belong to is taboo. I no longer fight with myself about who I am culturally, as I know now that pigeon-holing myself is limiting and that intersectionality matters, so I'm happy with being a mishmash of cultures. I've lived with multiple partners without being married, including Santosh. I love to drink booze, dance on speakers, wear short skirts, and do all kinds of other things that Indian aunties and uncles would be horrified about. But I couldn't care less about being the talk of the town.

I try not to self-silence or self-censor unless I want to do this, as part of my Adapted Self. I've encased myself with clouds who inspire me to be my Authentic Self as much as possible and who hold space for me when I'm hurting. I'm focused on using healing practices and my core wisdom to help me heal the trauma that lives in my body, mind, and soul.

Finally, I constantly remind myself that even though I have bad and ugly in me, I still get to belong.

This said, let me tell you, I don't do any of this flawlessly. I still wrestle with my demons. I constantly feel overwhelmed and exhausted. And just when I think "Oh, I'm healed!" something will happen that reminds me of how I'm still grappling with my Performing Self mask and my PPA armor.

But it's all good. Because I'm trying. I'm showing up. I'm giving it my best. I'm already living a life that, while still bumpy, is more joyful, authentic, and filled with belonging than my past. And this is beautiful.

The same can be true for you. You can choose to try, show up, give it your best, and be gentle and patient with yourself as you feel the beauty of belonging take you over.

$$\equiv$$

As I walk down the few steps, there's a handful of lawyers from the firm I'm presenting to hovering by the side of the stage waiting to speak to me. I just gave a talk about the importance of being who we are for ourselves, and how authenticity is a key ingredient for creating a more empowered and inclusive society. For many reasons, it's a message I deeply believe in.

One by one, as I chat with those who've been waiting, I feel my soul fill with gratitude. I'm genuinely touched by moments where I get to connect with people who so openheartedly share their joy, pain, wins, and struggles in life. It affirms that I'm not alone in feeling all that I do. And it's also a reminder of how we all want to belong.

I give the final person a hug, and I'm about to slip out of the room when the senior leader who invited me to speak comes up to me with a small piece of paper in his hand.

"Ritu, I thought you might want to see this," he says, waving the note gently in the air. "Someone from the audience slipped this to me. I asked and they said I could pass it along to you."

I take the note from his hand and, as I read the words, my eyes start to water. It says:

> "I saw Ritu speak about five years ago. She was stilted, and I wasn't looking forward to this session. Now, she is bringing her whole self, and she is wonderful. Thank you."

When I was younger, I worried that if I revealed my Authentic Self to the world, love would be taken away. I had no idea choosing to think this way was hurting my ability to connect with myself and with others—and ultimately, to belong. Now I'm receiving love for being all of me, and I'm reminded every day of how important it is to choose belonging.

TAKE A MOMENT TO REFLECT

How do belonging and authenticity come together for you in your life?

When do you feel safe to be your Authentic Self? Around whom does this happen? What does your authentic behavior look like? How does it make you feel? How does it impact your sense of belonging?

When do you show up as your Adapted Self? Around whom does this happen? What does your adaptive behavior look like? How does it make you feel? How does it impact your sense of belonging?

Are you aware of when you're flowing between your Authentic Self and Adaptive Self? How can you use healing practices and your core wisdom to live more as your Authentic Self?

What will you do going forward to be more of your Authentic Self? What choices will you make? How will you behave differently?

Questions for You to Explore Across All Chapters:

What are the key insights you've picked up from reading this chapter?

Which stories or messages most resonated with you? Why?

What are one or two things you'll do differently going forward?

CHAPTER ELEVEN

LET OTHERS BE MEAN WHILE YOU STAND IN YOUR POWER

t's early morning and a workday. I've just woken up, and rather than meditating, journaling, or intention-setting, I'm doing one of my favorite morning
routines: I'm in bed rabbit-holing on Instagram watching videos. Today I've
decided to focus on DIY facial massage techniques using a roller.

I can feel an anxious thumping inside me, signaling "get the hell up and be on
time for work for a change," especially since I'm in the thick of writing this book
and the deadline clock is ticking. This is what's leading me to toggle between
massage techniques and my work email every few minutes.

I'm about ten minutes away from becoming a professional facialist when I flip
over to my work inbox. And that's when I see the message come in from one of my
team members. It basically says I was profiled by Fox News on one of their shows
last night, our platforms are now overflowing with hate mail, and there's a link
to watch the video. Equal parts wanting to massage my face, having to pee badly,
and now feeling great panic, I click on the link and my mouth drops at the sight.

Picture this: in the top right-hand corner of the screen, there's an image of me
in a white sweatshirt that reads "I am The Revolution." I'm smiling so wide you

can see almost every single one of my teeth. At the bottom of the screen, there's a banner with the words "Exposing the 'DEI' Racket." The rest of the frame is filled by Laura Ingraham, host of the Fox News primetime show *The Ingraham Angle*, a fan favorite among millions of right-wing viewers.

As I watch the clip, I start to laugh. In it, the host, who shall no longer be named, introduces me, mispronounces my name, sarcastically describes the work my company does, and plays a snippet from one of my YouTube videos where I talk about anti-racism. She then lashes out at me with a string of insults, which include calling attention to my use of "a lot of hand movements." She even mockingly acts out my supposed gestures by chaotically wiggling her hands in the air—her own version of spirit fingers.

It's utterly ridiculous. And I don't care one bit about what she thinks or has to say about me. But that's not the issue. The problem is that, while my bit of the almost ten-minute segment lasts about a minute and a half, that's all it takes for the racist-sexist-oppressive Fox News fan base and other haters to come for me. For months and months and months, and even now, across a range of channels, I get all kinds of ugly messages.

I'm called a range of foul names I can't repeat here, or kids won't be able to open this book. I'm also informed of my perceived value on this planet, like "You're not wanted," and "You will destroy this country because you're not White," and "You need to move back to the third world country you came from," and "I hope you and your entire family become homeless and your disgusting business goes bankrupt."

Delightful.

Here's what I know to be true: they come for me because they want to stop me. To silence me. To push me down. To punish me. But what they don't know is that, even as I sit there in bed with my mouthguard still in, holding my pee and wishing I'd given myself a facial massage instead of clicking on the Fox News link, I'm committed to being disruptive in all I do.

I may not have felt this before, but I sure as hell do now: I am a warrior princess with revolutionary blood running through my veins. Nothing can stop me from setting free my greatness, speaking my truth, living and being my best, and reaching for the stars—because this is what my path to belonging now looks like.

And I don't want anything to stop you either.

Here's the thing: when we showcase our authenticity and claim the belonging we rightfully deserve, sometimes the meanies, haters, trolls, and anyone else who can't handle it will come for us. They emerge from inside our families and friend crews; they can be well-intentioned beloveds who have no idea of their hurtful impact; they're colleagues in the workplace; and they can even be random people. They want to tear us down for a whole host of misguided reasons: we speak the truth and they can't take it; we seem too joyful and anchored, while they're not; our skirts are too short or, worse yet, we have no right to wear a skirt; we grew up in the wrong neighborhood; we ought not love and/or have sex with the people we do; we don't have enough money or education; our bloodlines aren't good enough; our accents are bad; our faiths are evil; our hair is too long, our hair is too short, our hair is too curly, our hair is all over us, or insert-the-issue-with-our-hair; and so much more.

Some of the people who come for us are angry, nasty, and vengeful to their core, while others are sad, wounded, and unhealed. Yes, they hate on us and may actually hate us. But what's really happening is that they hate themselves more than they hate us. In fact, the main reason they're hating on us is that they don't love themselves—which is a huge insight and takeaway for us all.

> " Tearing others down will never bring us deep-rooted joy. It may give us a temporary lift, but it's harmful to use this as a way to fill our "joy cup."

Rather than creating sweet belonging in their lives, they're choosing to lift themselves up by tearing others down. They want to manipulate, gaslight, and block others so that it'll help them feel better about their own struggles—because they're experiencing moments of darkness and they're badly hurting. And, both knowingly and unknowingly, they want to drag us into their toxicity. They want us to rip at others as well. And we may be drawn into doing this.

But remember: tearing others down will never bring us deep-rooted joy. It may give us a temporary lift, but it's harmful to use this as a way to fill our "joy cup." In getting sucked into this toxic whirlwind, we'll constantly need to criticize and pit ourselves against others, which will only expand our wounds. It'll never bump us up. It'll never heal us. And it'll never lead to true belonging.

Given this, we don't want to be like them. We don't need to be like them. We've got great strength within us. And this is what we need to tap into in these types of moments instead. We want to stand in our power, which is exactly what I'm going to do as I jump out of bed.

It's going to be a wild day, but at least I know I've got this.

≡

Along your path to belonging, learning to stand in your power is everything. And, in saying this, I'm talking about standing in your *personal* power, instead of your social power.

It's your personal power that unleashes experiences of belonging for you. It compels you to embrace your authenticity and reveal it to the world; to use your voice to offer your thoughts and speak your mind; to claim opportunities you deserve; and to demand you be treated with equity, respect, and humanity. Which is why you must focus on growing your personal power.

The challenge in prioritizing personal power is that the allure of social power is strong. But, as I'll share with you now, it just won't bring about belonging like your personal power will.

> This chapter delves into the transformative impact personal power can have on your journey to unlock belonging.

SOCIAL POWER IS A HOUSE OF CARDS

Social power is about the heightened status we hold in society as a result of our job and title, our cultural identities, how much money and education we have, where we were born, the languages we speak and how we speak them, and much more. It's based on a flawed system of supremacy over others, which means it pits people against each other. And if that's not troubling enough, it's entirely externally focused and determined, in that others get to decide our worth. They shape how much power we get because of who we are and what we have, and they also get to decide when our power can be taken away. Because of this, our social power goes up or down depending on the situation we're in, while affirming inequities in society. It strikes at what belonging is about.

Given all of what's happening in our world right now, social power matters a lot and it's especially noticeable when we don't have it. This is why many of us have run around collecting degrees, awards, money, and possessions. But here's my truth: yes, I feel a bit of security and confidence because I hold some social power. That said, since social power is so problematic, I'm tremendously uncomfortable about it. I'm well aware that because it's rooted in ranking people's worthiness against my own, my social power is directly tied to the control and dominance I have over others who don't have it. And, of course, I hate this stratification. It's the reason I do the work I do.

Instead of chasing social power, we want to cultivate endless personal power within us. It's what we need for deep-rooted anchoring and belonging in life.

$$=$$

As I open the door to Mama's nursing home room and take a few steps inside, I can see Thesa, her caregiver, sitting next to the bed. She's feeding Mama lunch. I linger quietly at the door, not wanting to interrupt this moment.

Thesa brings a glass to her mouth. "Mama," she coos in a loving voice, "it's apple juice. You love apple juice."

Mama smiles at Thesa in response and then takes a few sips.

"Mmmm," she says to Thesa. Very slowly, Mama reaches out her hand to pull Thesa's head in close and gives her a few kisses on her forehead. I can hear the smacking sound her lips make from across the room. Then they both start to giggle.

Mama loves Thesa. And Thesa loves Mama.

I marvel at the tenderness and affection that flow between them. But I'm also struck by Thesa's powerful presence. It's not the mighty, in-your-face force field

I've become used to during my decades in the business and legal world. It's a calm, subtle, and luminous energy that I can't help but be drawn to. It's so rare to be in the company of such light and grace, I wonder if one of the reasons I visit Mama during Thesa's shifts is so that I can be around her. I feel like a cat wanting to rub up against her leg.

Over time, Thesa and I tell each other all about our own lives. I take her through my family's story and my own journey, and she hangs on to every word as I share. She tells me about her humble beginnings back home in the Philippines, and the challenges and blessings that came with immigrating to Canada. She talks about how hard it is to be respected as an immigrant in her profession. She gives me details about her beautiful family, including their ups and downs. And she opens up about her experiences helping the elderly at the end of their lives as they slowly move toward passing and then eventually do. She reveals that even when they can barely talk, as is the case now with Mama Bhasin, they still speak with her. I learn more from her about the end of life than I have from anyone else.

Thesa is just a few years older than I am, but I've come to see her as a sage. I repeatedly ask about how she's developed her quiet but incredible strength. Every time, she humbly smiles and shrugs, then tells me, "This is just me." And as an expert on the Performing Self, I know she's not just feeding me lines. I also know that Thesa has a deep well of core wisdom: she puts effort into taking care of her body, mind, and soul; she's deeply mindful and spiritual; she surrounds herself with clouds; and she chooses to have a positive and peaceful mindset.

Thesa often comes to mind when I'm meeting with senior leaders from across a range of industries. I interact with many people with high social power given their job, affluence, networks, and cultural identities—many of whom I can tell are both unhappy and delicate. I can smell it a mile away. When something throws them off balance given how hard life can be, some of them start to fall apart. It's a reminder that just because some people have lots of social power doesn't mean they have lots of personal power. And the reverse is also true. Some people may not have high social power, but they can be filled with tremendous personal power—like Thesa.

This is yet another reason why my heart is filled with love and respect for Thesa: she knows who she is, she embraces her essence, and she gracefully puts her energy out into the world. Thesa emanates belonging in all she does, and I'm learning from her.

We find our teachers in different souls.

As I put my purse on the table in Mama's room, the clanging sound causes Thesa to turn around. She smiles brightly when she sees me. And like a magnet, I'm immediately pulled into her light.

This is the radiance of personal power.

YOUR PERSONAL POWER UNLEASHES BELONGING

Personal power is about recognizing our beauty and worth based on what's inside us. It's about honoring our authenticity, purpose, values, beliefs, unique characteristics, cultures, skills, and goodness. It's about having a calm, settled, and resilient body and mind. It doesn't have anything to do with anyone else—it's about our relationship with ourselves. It's about us loving ourselves to our core. It's about belonging to ourselves.

It's also about having a mindset that's anchored in knowing that our self-work, dedication, and resilience will help us to heal, grow, develop, and thrive in all we do. That, as the captain of our own ship, we both choose and create our own joy. It's about recognizing that our internal locus of control is far more valuable than focusing externally. And, because of this, personal power is healing.

> Instead of chasing social power, we want to cultivate endless personal power within us. It's what we need for deep-rooted anchoring and belonging in life.

When we have lots of personal power, we're anchored. We accept that the path to belonging is filled with both beautiful *and* hard moments. We know that good stuff and bad stuff can swirl around us (think: this too shall pass), but we stay rooted in who we are. We're like a rock foundation in the face of bad experiences. Yes, we hurt, but we still feel solid. We come to a place where we feel less and less shame, and we no longer want to avert our eyes. We're done with our mask, armor, and stage. Instead, we deal with people, situations, opportunities, possibilities, issues, challenges, and barriers head-on because we feel unstoppable. This is why personal power is essential to finding belonging.

Because personal power comes from within—we don't have to go to others for it—it's unshakable. We can go from situation to situation and retain our personal power. No one can take it away from us without our consent, so we're always directly in control of how much we have, and we can keep growing it. Sure, it'll ebb and flow based on what's happening to us in life, but, even then, we own how much we have. And because of this, it gives us tremendous peace, assurance, confidence, and freedom.

Personal power is directly linked to our core wisdom. To grow it, we want to focus on using the same practices we talked about in *Healing* that help build our core wisdom. From breathwork techniques, movement-based rituals, and vibration-based experiences to touch-centric activities, mindfulness moments, and holistic-health habits, all these practices work to expand our personal power.

Recall, our efforts to be embodied and intentional help us to clock and name what we're sensing inside us; let go of energy and negativity we're holding; be more settled even during difficult moments; and interrupt and replace the negative messages we hold with loving beliefs about who we are. All of this leads us to cultivate self-love and self-compassion, believe in our abilities, be authentic, take space with our presence, insist on respect for who we are, and know we have every right to use our voice when we want to—which is what personal power is all about.

To be clear, standing in our personal power isn't about being in a permanent state of happiness, because again, that doesn't exist. When we have heightened personal power, we know that both life and the path to belonging are about having more moments of joy, feeling connected to our values and who we are, and understanding what our life's purpose is.

Of course, when we have lots of personal power, we'll have many more moments of joy and belonging. And that's why personal power is so important along your bumpy and curvy path in life.

=

I'm standing in a long, winding airport security line after doing a big talk in New York City. I'm feeling a mix of excitement, relief, and exhaustion, plus I'm craving a long shower and my bed. To pass the time as I wait, I'm playing around on my phone.

"You can move up, you know!" a man's voice barks at me.

His almost-screaming tone pulls me out of texting and causes me to jump out of my skin.

I whip around to check out the dragon that's breathing fire at me and come face to face with a tall White man in a well-tailored business suit. He's not the only one who looks like this; I'm surrounded by this archetype in line. I would've looked more like them too, only I swapped out my "speaker outfit"—a business dress and heels—for a denim onesie and sneakers the second I got to the airport. I did this in a bathroom stall, where my clothing contortionism skills came in handy.

I sigh.

I'm so tired of being hassled by some businessman types when I'm at the airport. Some of them constantly question me about why I'm standing in Zone 1 to board the plane or cut me off in lines or overtake the shared storage space under the seats in front of us. Whether they intend to or not, their actions shout "You don't belong," and, of course, it stings.

This time, I suppose I'm the culprit. It's before the pandemic, and I'm leaving four-foot gaps in the line because I'm distracted by my phone. I know it's annoying, but is it bad enough to yell at a random stranger in line?! No. Not unless your social power makes you think you can.

I think back to moments in the past where random high-social-powered people out in the world spoke rudely to me. The wind would be knocked right out of me, and I couldn't bring myself to speak. But hours later, I'd find myself writing an Oscar-winning rebuttal and then delivering it in the bathroom mirror.

That was before I doubled-tripled-quadrupled down on living a life of belonging by doing my healing work and building my core wisdom. I'm filled with so much more personal power now, so this time, I'm ready. I'm committed to asserting my right to belong, and I'm not going to let anyone take that away from me.

I've even scripted for this type of moment.

I look him dead in the eyes and loudly, but calmly, ask, "Are you speaking to me?"

"Yes, I am!" he growls back.

I stare at him silently for a few seconds. Then I say these exact words in the same loud, firm, and calm tone: "That was upsetting. You can speak to me. But if you're going to do that, you must do so with respect."

His eyes suddenly widen, his face starts to turn tomato red, and, while his mouth drops wide open, not a word comes out. I continue to look at him silently. He turns away. As I slowly turn forward to go back to analyzing my phone screen, I catch the stares of a bunch of people. Several women are smiling at me and nodding their heads, as are a few of the businessman types, while other men have the same deer-in-headlights look as the man behind me.

My hope is that they all remember this moment as clearly as I do.

I'm Ritu Bhasin, and no one gets to speak to me that way anymore.

TAKE A MOMENT TO REFLECT

How does it feel to know you hold social power? What sensations and feelings come up inside you? What thoughts go through your mind?

On the flip side, how does it feel to know you hold personal power? What sensations and feelings come up inside you? What thoughts go through your mind?

In which situations do you most feel your personal power? Why do you think that is? How does your personal power impact your sense of belonging? Your joy in life?

What healing practices will you use going forward to grow your personal power? Why is this important to you?

Who around you has heightened personal power? How can you tap into their energy to inspire you to grow your personal power?

Questions for You to Explore Across All Chapters:

What are the key insights you've picked up from reading this chapter?

Which stories or messages most resonated with you? Why?

What are one or two things you'll do differently going forward?

CHAPTER TWELVE

CLAIMING YOUR BELONGING

I'm on a video call with two White C-suite leaders of a company to talk about the upcoming unconscious bias presentation they've hired me to do for them. It's July 2020. Between the stress of the pandemic, the social inequities that are surfacing right now, the pain of George Floyd's murder, and the workload I have as a DEI professional, my ability to remain calm in the face of racism is at an all-time low. And this conversation hits a record high for offensive behaviors during a client meeting.

It starts off with the chief operating officer, a White woman, cheerfully saying, "It's nice to meet you, Ree-too!" when we first get onto Zoom. Name mispronunciation aside, normally this greeting would be fine. But this time, the words burn.

"Actually, we've met before," I reply in a voice about five octaves higher, which is what happens when I'm upset—I become very high-pitched. I continue, "Two weeks ago? When we met by video to discuss this engagement?"

Silence.

Blinking furiously as she stares at me on the screen, she stammers, "Oh... ahhh... ummm... Yes. I must have gotten confused from watching one of your DEI videos."

Really?!

This leader had actively sought me out to teach about interrupting racial oppression during a historic moment in the fight against racism. She'd found me online, watched some of my videos, sent a flattering email about how she wanted to work with my company, and scheduled two calls with me. So, when she forgets who I am, even though she interviewed me by video for thirty minutes two weeks before *and* I had corrected her pronunciation of my name back then too *and* she's been emailing me for days about our work together leading up to this call *and* she doesn't offer me a proper apology, only a flimsy response? It feels like a back-handed slap across my Brown-girl face. It's a slap I'm already familiar with, but it stings every time, nevertheless.

It's a reminder of how I'm invisible for some.

No matter how hard I've worked to overcome a system designed against me; the impact of the work I'm doing to create change; my passion and goodness; all my awards, accolades, and distinctions; the hundreds of thousands of people I've presented to globally; the thousands of people I've directly coached—none of that matters. My name, my face, my voice, and my work all can be erased. I can still be made to feel like I don't belong. It's no wonder I'm rattled.

I want to say something to her. But, of course, The Voice shouts back, *You can't do that! She's the client.* I decide not to say anything. But I know I need to do something, or I won't be a well-adjusted human for the remainder of the call. So I dig into my core wisdom treasure chest and I start to belly breathe, which is a good thing because this call will go from bad to worse. With one tokenistic comment after another, it's becoming obvious I'm being hired for performative reasons. It feels like they just want to tick a box showing they've "done something" in response to the racial justice movement, and they want to use me as their puppet.

To confirm my suspicion, I quickly jump to asking about what content they want me to focus on in my session. And this is when the chief operating officer utters the following words: "We'd like you to focus on how People of Color have racial biases too."

To be clear, she doesn't say this after requesting that I teach White people about their racial biases or naming other pressing concepts. She essentially leads with this. I'm stunned. And I can feel rage pounding through me.

Barely holding it together, I bluntly tell her that if she wants me to talk about the racial biases People of Color hold, I first need to teach about the concept of white supremacy. I might as well have said, as part of this work, I'm going to have to burn down her house. Her eyes practically pop out of their sockets, and she stammers something like, "No, we don't want you to talk about that."

I've had enough.

In my mind, I hear myself declare, "This is so frogging wrong! I have to say something." And this time I'm ready for The Voice. The lid to my treasure chest is now open, and I'm rolling around in my core wisdom. Before The Voice can say anything again, I call upon one of my favorite affirmations and I tell myself, "Ritu Bhasin, stand in your power! If you don't say something here, who will?!"

Then, I take a big belly breath, I open my mouth, and I let out a version of the language I've scripted for moments like these when people treat me in hateful ways and I want to assert my belonging by calling out the offensive behavior.

I start off by saying something to the effect of "I want you to know that I'm feeling very upset and activated right now. I feel disrespected by..." and I name a few things that offended me. I also say, "I feel like racial bias is at play here because..." and I rattle off a list of the garbage I just went through.

> " When others diminish or reject you on the basis of who you are, they strike at your sense of belonging. While you can't control their actions, you can always choose to belong to yourself. Through your actions, you can choose to claim belonging for *yourself* with *yourself*.

As I speak, I can feel my voice quiver and my hands shake, so I sit up straighter as I keep taking belly breaths, and I soothingly rub my hands against my legs—all to signal to my body and mind that I'm safe.

I deliberately choose to avoid saying "I think you're being racist" and "This whole experience screams of white supremacy" because, given their fragility, I know they won't be able to handle this type of directness. But I'm not fussed about this. What I care about is that even my toned-down language feels so empowering to share. I tapped into my core wisdom and used my voice to call out their disrespect and claim my belonging. It feels amazing.

Another choice I make is to *not* apologize for what is coming out of my mouth. I don't say, "I'm sorry but I want you to know..." I don't say, "I'm so sorry if this is hard to hear." I'm intentional about this: I don't say the word "sorry" even once. I'm unapologetically unapologetic. Because I'm not sorry for anything I'm saying. It has to be said. I have every right to belong. And they need to know this.

When I finish speaking, unsurprisingly, the leaders look dumbfounded. They weren't expecting me to speak my truth. They do their best to muster up some words that sound like a half-hearted apology, and then they get the frog off the video call as quickly as they can. Immediately after I log off, I burst into tears and my body automatically starts to tremble, which makes sense, given how much stressful energy was just generated in my body. I cry and shake for a few minutes until it all slowly stops. And I keep using my healing practices and core wisdom to give my body, mind, and soul what they need over the days to come to get the negativity out of me and to settle my system.

Later in the day, they'll email to fire me, and I won't bat an eyelash. Because that's not what matters to me. What I care about is that I experienced belonging with my own soul. Their racist behavior was a denial of who I am and of my identities. But I showed up for myself by standing in my personal power, using my voice, speaking my truth, and communicating that I rejected their treatment of me.

And in doing so, I claimed belonging for myself.

It's a life lesson that comes from the heart of this book: when others diminish or reject you on the basis of who you are, they strike at your sense of belonging. While you can't control their actions, you can always choose to belong to yourself. Through your actions, you can choose to claim belonging for *yourself* with *yourself*.

When you're a kid, it's hard to assert your right to belong because you don't tend to have much agency over how you live. Your elders control most of your moves. But as an adult, the magical world of making your own decisions opens up and you get to exercise control over a bunch of choices: who you want to be, how you want to behave, who you want to be around, who you want to love, how you want to be treated, where you want to draw boundaries, and how you want to experience belonging.

While you may not be able to control exactly what comes your way, like the hardships you experience, you still have agency over how you behave. No matter what happens to you in life, you always have the power of choice. Even in the deepest, darkest, and most difficult moments, you can still choose to prioritize your core wisdom, reframe how you view the situation, and respond differently than you normally would to how you're being treated.

> This chapter discusses the importance of choosing to claim your belonging, especially when hurtful experiences come your way, and lays out strategies to help you make this happen.

CHOOSING TO UNLOCK BELONGING

To experience greater belonging, especially in the face of hurtful and hateful things coming your way, you'll want to behave differently going forward—particularly if your old ways of doing things haven't been giving you the feelings of acceptance and empowerment you're looking for. But sometimes we don't know where to start, what our options are, or whether we can even be different going forward. We don't trust ourselves.

If this is you, know you're not alone. So many people feel this way at times, myself included. But here are a few important points to keep in mind to inspire you to make different choices going forward:

1. **The brain is plastic, so you can change your wiring, which then impacts how you behave, at any time or age.** That old saying "you can't teach an old dog new tricks" is wrong. Your brain is malleable until the day you die. When you change your thoughts, you can create new pathways in your brain, leading to fresh ways of showing up. In

a nutshell, you can change how you're behaving to experience more belonging if you want to.

2. **Your core wisdom will help you to see you have more agency over how you behave than you think you do.** Your core wisdom will help you to stand more in your personal power, which in turn will lead you to seek out greater belonging. And, because of this, you'll come to learn you have more control over claiming belonging than you initially thought you did.

3. **You must get clear on why you want to change how you're living and what outcomes you desire from making different decisions.** When you deeply understand your drivers for craving belonging and have awareness of the benefits you'll enjoy, you'll be more likely to adjust how you're acting. Simply put, you want to anchor to the *why* and the *what* to help unlock more belonging in your life.

But even when you identify with these points, you may not know how to act or what to say to claim your belonging in a situation when a hurtful thing happens. Picture a moment when someone has said something very upsetting to you and you want to handle it in a more empowered way, but instead you freeze and become speechless, only to find yourself coming up with an award-winning sermon hours later.

Or maybe there are moments where you know exactly what you want to say or do, but you can't bring yourself to make that happen because of fear. Maybe The Voice is filling your mind with messages like "don't speak" or "you can't do that" or "see, you're such a loser." Or you're worried that people will judge you. These reactions can feel so deflating.

To enjoy greater belonging going forward, you'll want to be more mindful and deliberate about planning out how to behave differently. And you'll also want to be primed and prepared for moments when feeling like you belong is particularly important.

To make this happen, here's an exercise you can use to claim your belonging: imagine the types of difficult experiences you typically fear. Pick one of these moments to start off with and play it out in your mind: what might happen, where you might be, what might be said, who might be involved, and what other details matter to you. Now, ask yourself:

- In the past, when I've found myself in a situation like this, what did I feel in my body and mind?
- How did this situation impact me?

As you reflect on your answers, use your core wisdom practices to help settle and release any sensations, emotions, energy, and thoughts that come up inside you. Then, give thought to how you'd like to behave the next time you're in this situation to claim your belonging. Ask yourself:

- How do I want to show up differently?
- What words do I want to say out loud in that moment?
- How do I want to act?
- Which affirmations will I use to encourage myself to speak and act?
- Which core wisdom practices will I leverage to help settle my body and mind?

Finally, close your eyes and picture yourself speaking and acting based on how you answered these questions. To help you remain calm as you do, use some of your favorite core wisdom practices, like deep breathing or holding your heart or doing a quick body scan or humming. Play the situation out in your mind moment by moment, capturing every detail.

In taking you through these steps, I'm essentially highlighting the power of scripting, self-coaching, and visualization, all of which can be added to your core wisdom treasure chest to help you experience heightened love and acceptance.

Scripting is the act of planning in advance what you want to say in tough situations, since the stress in the moment may cause you to shut down. With scripting, you write out what you would want to say in a difficult moment. Then you practice saying what you've written down again and again and again so that the words are stored in your brain for future retrieval.

I love scripting because it helps to create an assertive response you can use to stand in your power and claim your belonging. I use it all the time, from conversations with racist clients to offensive moments at the airport. Check out the language I share with you in these stories (and the next story coming up about me and my Dad), because my scripts may help you to come up with your own versions you can use when someone's hurtful behavior is striking at your ability to belong.

But despite scripting the heck out of situations, sometimes I still don't feel safe or comfortable enough to speak. And that's okay. I'm doing my best to honor where my body and mind are at any given time. Depending on the experience, and if I feel up for it, I can always go back later and share what I wanted to say. You don't always have to speak in the actual moment.

Self-coaching is the practice of using pre-selected words of encouragement and guidance to inspire you to speak and act in tough situations when your mind is filled with negative self-talk. Not only does self-coaching help to reduce stress and build your confidence, but similar to breathwork and body scans, it's easy to do, you don't need anyone's help to make it happen, and you can do it anywhere. Basically, you pick some positive, affirming words like "I'm worthy of belonging" or "I've got this" that can be used during a self-delivered pep talk when you're feeling afraid to say or do something.

Visualization is what a basketball player does when she's off the court and imagining her best shot. You picture, in detail, how you want to behave down the road when difficult moments arise. You fill your mind with images, colors, sounds, words, smells, and whatever else is important, and you play out the scenarios repeatedly. It's a lot like scripting, in that you're conditioning your brain by embedding it with future behavior.

My favorite spot to practice visualization is when I'm in the shower or swimming in the ocean. I have all kinds of wondrous visions while I'm taking in the sound and feel of water, not to mention being shut off from the world helps me focus.

> " There's a way out of constantly feeling inferior and unworthy: it's through the power of choosing to behave in ways that help you to experience greater belonging.

With the power of scripting, self-coaching, and visualization added to your list of empowerment strategies, you're ready for the next time a situation arises where you want to assert yourself to claim belonging. In that moment, reach into your core wisdom treasure chest for practices to calm yourself, self-coach to help you take action, and use your scripts to speak your truth. Then, in the days and weeks that follow, rely on healing practices to help settle and release any sensations, emotions, energy, and thoughts coming up inside you.

This may sound granular and calculated, but it's these types of strategies that help us along our journey to heal and to belong. For those of you who often feel like you're trapped in a dark tunnel, my hope is you'll now see there's a way out of constantly feeling inferior and unworthy: it's through the power of choosing to behave in ways that help you to experience greater belonging.

No more averting our spirit.

No more suppressing our authenticity.

No more clinging to a mask, armor, and stage.

Not when we can choose to claim our belonging.

≡

My father and I are sitting at a booth at a restaurant near my mother's nursing home. It's become our "spot." While I now see him once a week while visiting Mama, our one-on-one time over these lunches is special.

We try our best to minimize talking about the painful journey we're on as caregivers, since this already dominates our calls and messages each week. Instead, we focus on the new life he's building as he finds his legs as an eighty-year-old turban-wearing Punjabi-Canadian man who's navigating an ever-changing, dynamic, and difficult world. We chat about everything from his childhood memories, the new recipes he's trying out, and the gossip in his Indian social circles to why he'd rather play bridge at the practically all-White seniors' center with the relaxed men's group over the finicky women's group. The more we bond in this way, the more I'm struck by how much I'm like him and how much I like him.

My discipline, work ethic, verbosity, bad temper, stubbornness, and ride-or-die spirit, all of this I get from Papa Bhasin. I am my father's daughter, even though for years I wished I wasn't. Along the winding road of our relationship, we've been like oil and water. This was especially the case in my late thirties and early forties when I started to live more authentically and draw boundaries around where his feedback isn't welcome anymore. Like, on anything related to my appearance. I don't want to hear about how much he hates my nose ring or my new tan or the wild patterns I wear. Or how loud I laugh or how animated my face is. Or anything to do with my love life. I definitely don't want to listen to his commentary on that.

It's an adjustment for him, and he doesn't take it well. But I don't really give him a choice, if he wants to maintain a connection with me. And frankly, in areas where he still deeply believes he has the right to be forceful, he is. He's also given me feedback about how I've been showing up. He tells me he doesn't appreciate that I'm constantly tense about work when I'm with him. It makes me feel like he can't relax around me. He shares that he wishes I'd be more open to listening to him vent about his life stresses, which I normally shut down because of the level of negativity. And he says it feels like I constantly want to argue with him.

He's not wrong. So I'm trying to make changes. We're resetting the dynamics in our relationship so that we can both finally experience belonging with each other, which feels both beautiful *and* hard. It's taking a lot of blood, sweat, and tears to reach a healthy "new normal." But we're getting there, bit by bit, and as this continues to unfold, the more I understand, appreciate, and adore him. Especially since this is all happening as he cares for Mama. In moments, I'm in awe of him. I don't know another man from his generation and cultural upbringing who shows up like he does.

And this is why these hangouts are so important: we get to choose how to rewire our relationship as father and daughter.

At this lunch, he's just finished monologuing about the great deals he's been finding at Costco lately, when he turns to talking about something to do with Mama's care. It's an area where sometimes we don't see eye to eye, and the Taurus/bull in him and the Leo/lioness in me butt heads. Hard.

"Dad, I don't think we should do that," I tell him calmly, but I already notice a stern vibe take over my tone.

He comes back at me with a salty response, and the game is on. We're now politely bickering back and forth and trying to do this as civilly as possible, given we're in public, and because "What will society think?!" if they hear us. We should've just stuck to talking about the pricing of frozen avocados and canned tuna, two of my favorite Costco items.

I've just given him a harsh retort to something he's said, when five words come out of his mouth that send shivers down my spine: "Oh, Ritu, you're so difficult."

Those. Words.

He went there.

As a strong and feisty girl growing up, I lost count of how many times he used wording like this with me. It cut then, and it still does because it makes me feel like there's something wrong with my passionate spirit. Like I'm broken and he wants to highlight this. Like it makes him love me less. Like in his eyes I don't deserve to belong.

For about three seconds, the fighter in me wants to lash out at him, something I've done many times before, because it feels safer and easier to do than to name my pain. Of course, being fiery with him rarely goes well and usually ends up in a standoff that can last a few weeks. I've often done it anyway, despite knowing that a deadlock would happen, because sometimes being a warrior hasn't been enough. I've needed to be a gladiator.

But this time, I choose to take the opposite path: I don't take him on. My core wisdom is signaling that I need to be different in this moment—that I should stand in my power and claim my belonging in another way. So instead, I put a hand on my chest where I can now feel a throbbing and I let the tears start to flow. And then I call upon the words I've been practicing for moments like this when he says something hurtful to me.

I take a slow breath in and, as I exhale, I softly tell him, "That wasn't a very nice thing to say to me, Dad. That was a mean comment. It really hurts my feelings when you talk to me like that."

His eyes widen and, in what might be a first, it seems like he doesn't know what to say. We sit in silence for what feels like an eternity. He then gently replies, "I'm sorry. I'm very sorry, my Putri. I didn't know. Don't be upset." He reaches his big hand across the table and wipes a few of the tears that are rushing down my tiny cheeks. And, as he does, his eyes start to water.

As I sit quietly and look at my eighty-year-old father, my heart flutters with love and appreciation. In this moment of belonging, I feel seen by him and it's very moving for me, especially after all we've been through together. In my mind I think, "Wow, we have come a long way." Never could I have imagined that a time would come when rather than silence my voice, or fight fire with fire, I'd vulnerably choose to share my hurt with my father *and* he'd actually honor what I'm saying. In fact, for many years, I've held back from taking this approach. But this time I was ready to be open and he was ready to receive.

> **The beautiful *and* hard path to belonging isn't a destination. It's a journey.**

This moment, and others like it, remind me of why expressing how we want to be treated—or choosing to claim belonging for ourselves—matters. It affirms why our core wisdom is so important for claiming our belonging and taking in the warm feelings that come up when it happens.

And it highlights two key takeaways: we can honor our parents while asserting our right to belong; these actions can coexist. And we can choose to create more belonging for ourselves and for others at any time in life, even at the age of eighty.

Because the beautiful *and* hard path to belonging isn't a destination. It's a journey.

TAKE A MOMENT TO REFLECT

In which situations or areas of your life do you want to claim greater belonging? Why is this? What is it about these moments that leads you to want to behave differently?

Are you already scripting for difficult moments to claim your belonging? What are some of the scripts you're using? What scripts will you create to leverage going forward?

How are you using self-coaching to claim your belonging? What are some of the affirmations or words you're using? What language will you add to your list of affirmations?

How are you using visualization to help claim your belonging? Where do you find it most effective to practice visualization? How will you leverage visualization in the future?

Questions for You to Explore Across All Chapters:

What are the key insights you've picked up from reading this chapter?

Which stories or messages most resonated with you? Why?

What are one or two things you'll do differently going forward?

CHAPTER THIRTEEN

THERE'S NOTHING WRONG WITH YOU AND THERE NEVER WAS

A s I stare at the boxes on the screen, I think to myself, "This is so strange and so wonderful, all at once." I've never done group therapy before, or anything like this virtually. But we're deep into the pandemic and this format makes sense. Plus, I need this support right now.

I'm juggling being there for my Mom, my Dad, all my other beloveds, my team, my clients, my business, every random person out there, and even the dust mites in the corners of my condo. Of course, the being that needs my attention the most and is getting the least is me. Despite all I have learned—all I have shown to you in these pages—it's tough to take care of myself when I have so little fuel in the tank. But I'm doing my best, which is why I keep showing up religiously for these sessions with my eight group members and our insightful therapist and elder.

Every time we meet, I eat up all that's being put in front of me as we focus on healing our wounds. We're a few months in now, and I'm already feeling lighter and freer to be me—both with them and in my life overall. It's another experience that's offering me beautiful belonging.

For the last while, we've been digging into our childhood trauma and sharing the hurtful childhood messages that still ring in our heads and hold us back. One by one we've been taking turns talking to our inner saboteur—a.k.a. The Voice—to basically declare, "I understand why you've become part of my life, but I don't need you anymore, thank you. I've got this."

Today is my turn.

In the chat board, I paste the list of the childhood messages I often still hear The Voice say to me. I give a few bullets, but one of them hurts the most: No one wants to be with you, be your friend, or choose you.

It's a reminder of how long this belief has been whirling in my mind.

One of the women from my group takes on the role of The Voice and slowly reads the messages out loud, while the others watch and hold space for me to just be. Though I've been listening to those words in my head my whole life, as I hear them come out of her mouth, my cheeks immediately start to burn, my belly fills with queasiness, and my eyes twitch like tears are on their way.

She pauses so that I have a chance to respond. As I begin talking to her, my voice shakes with both fear and determination. The Voice is so mean and nasty. And these messages still hurt so bad. Which is why I want to take The Voice on.

So I do.

For the next few minutes, I go back and forth, bantering with my inner saboteur to claim belonging for myself. And I don't hold back. My upset and anger over these words pour out of me, but I also feel a deep sense of strength and dignity, reflections of my personal power. The mix of feelings is intense and, unsurprisingly, the tears kick in. As I weep, I bury my face into the fluorescent-green cleaning cloth I've been using to dry my tears during our sessions. When I cry, I've found that using a soft cleaning rag is much better for my delicate skin than two-ply tissue, which both pulls at and gets stuck to my face.

I hear our elder gently say, "Ritu, how are you doing?"

I inhale and breathe out, "It's really good to let this out. But this is so hard."

She encourages me to pause, take a few more deep breaths, and look at my circle of resonance that's on the screen. I follow her words and take a moment to make eye contact with each group member in their little boxes.

"Ritu, will you try something?" my elder then asks. I nod my head.

"I'd like you to repeat these words." And then she says the following to me: "There's nothing wrong with me and there never was."

As I recite these words out loud, my chest flutters with the feeling of belonging.

My inner saboteur goes silent.

My body is tingly.

My eyes open wide.

My heart opens wide.

My mind opens wide.

My soul opens wide.

I've got this.

You've got this.

And together, we've got this.

KEEP GROWING: WORKS I LOVE

HEALING TRAUMA

My Grandmother's Hands: Racialized Trauma and the Pathway to Mending Our Hearts and Bodies
by Resmaa Menakem

What Happened to You? Conversations on Trauma, Resilience, and Healing
by Bruce D. Perry and Oprah Winfrey

Call of the Wild: How We Heal Trauma, Awaken Our Own Power, and Use It for Good
by Kimberly Ann Johnson

The Racial Healing Handbook: Practical Activities to Help You Challenge Privilege, Confront Systemic Racism, and Engage in Collective Healing
by Anneliese A. Singh, with Tim Wise and Derald Wing Sue

Healing through Words
by Rupi Kaur

LIVING WELL

The Body Is Not an Apology: The Power of Radical Self-Love
by Sonya Renee Taylor, with Ijeoma Oluo

Untamed
by Glennon Doyle

The Gifts of Imperfection: Let Go of Who You Think You're Supposed to Be and Embrace Who You Are
by Brené Brown

The Four Agreements: A Practical Guide to Personal Freedom
by Don Miguel Ruiz

BELONGING IN THE WORKPLACE

The Memo: What Women of Color Need to Know to Secure a Seat at the Table
by Minda Harts

The First, the Few, the Only: How Women of Color Can Redefine Power in Corporate America
by Deepa Purushothaman

How to Be an Ally: Actions You Can Take for a Stronger, Happier Workplace
by Melinda Briana Epler

FROM MY WORLD

If you want to keep digging into what I have to say about belonging, you'll find a range of self-reflection worksheets, exercises, blogs, videos, and practices at www.ritubhasin.com. And if you still want more, drop me a line to share your requests and feedback via Instagram at @ritu_bhasin or LinkedIn at in/ritubhasin. I love getting messages, so don't be shy!

For resources on belonging in the workplace, please visit my DEI consulting firm's site at www.bhasinconsulting.com. Here you'll find several tip sheets, articles, blogs, videos, and more on how to create organizational cultures that are rooted in authenticity and belonging. And if you'd like to learn more about our work, please reach out via our site. We'd love to hear from you.

GRATITUDE

Writing books does not come easy to me. In fact, let me be more direct: I think it's really frogging hard.

So much so that after writing *The Authenticity Principle*, I doubted I'd ever do it again. Which is why I deemed my first book's acknowledgments section "an epic soliloquy of love." (I actually said this in the first few paragraphs of the section!) I didn't think I'd find it in me to go through the hellish process of writing another book. But here we are, and I'm so grateful I did. And I now have another army of people to thank for their incredible support to get me here. But because I know better, this time I'm going to keep it short and sweet.

To my team at Random House Canada, and in particular to Amanda Ferreira, Sue Kuruvilla, and Kristin Cochrane, thank you for supporting me from the beginning and for your unyielding belief in me. I love what we have created!

And speaking of being there from the beginning, to my fabulous agent, Suzanne Brandreth, who I now hold in my heart as Suzanne Bhenji: I couldn't have pulled this off without you. To say I appreciate you would be an understatement. Thank you.

To my kick-ass team at Krupp Agency, and Darren Lisiten especially, thank you for being there by my side throughout this whirlwind of an experience.

To Naren Aryal, Myles Schrag, and the rest of the team at Amplify Publishing Group, you rock. Thank you for understanding who I am and working so hard to bring my vision to life.

To my team at bhasin consulting inc. (bci), there will never be enough words to express how much I appreciate all you do for me and bci's mission. Thank you for everything.

To all my early readers and advisors, thank you for your time, commitment, and feedback. My heart explodes with affection and appreciation for your support. To Rakhi Mutta and J to the G, there's extra love coming your way.

To my clients, advocates, and angels, every day I reflect on how blessed I am to have your collective support. My life is better because you believe in me. Thank you.

To my family, beloveds, "clouds," and Santosh specifically, I won't be able to capture in a few sentences just how much your love and support has mattered over this extremely difficult period. You've held me up when I felt like I was falling. For this, and much more, I'm so thankful. I love you all.

To my ancestors, as I walk in your footsteps and feel your warrior blood run through my veins, I'm holding my head high. Thank you for paving this incredible path for me.

My final thanks goes to the Divine, to Waheguru. *Sabna Jiya Ka Ek Data So Mai Visar Na Jaye*—Japji Sahib, Sri Guru Granth Sahib.

Lastly, I want to share a vision I keep having: I'm picturing Mama Bhasin holding this book in one hand while she pumps her other fist in the air and yells, "My daughter, the motivational speaker!" This makes me so happy. And makes this journey so worth it.

ABOUT THE AUTHOR

Ritu Bhasin, LL.B. MBA, is an award-winning speaker, author, and expert in belonging, equity, leadership, and empowerment, and is the CEO of bhasin consulting inc., a renowned DEI consulting firm that has worked with hundreds of organizations internationally.

A passionate advocate for living and leading authentically, Ritu has presented to hundreds of thousands globally and coached over a thousand professionals to cultivate and claim belonging. She's living proof of what can happen when you stand in your power while fighting the hate and hardships in your way.

But Ritu didn't always feel empowered to be an unapologetic, fiercely authentic person. Born in Toronto, Canada, to Sikh Punjabi immigrant parents, Ritu experienced the constant sting of racist bullying growing up, while also struggling with cultural tension about her identities. She carried her childhood trauma into adulthood, where she felt constant pressure to mask her authentic self across most of her relationships and in her work life, first as a lawyer and then as an HR leader at a global law firm.

While trying to convince herself that she was living the "dream," Ritu had a startling realization: because of relentless experiences with hate and life hardships, she was minimizing her authenticity to "fit in" among circles where she felt she didn't belong. And in doing so, she was profoundly unhappy.

Looking to transform her life through the power of healing, Ritu left her corporate job, launched her global DEI consulting firm, became a yoga and mindfulness practitioner and teacher, studied trauma and wellness healing practices, wrote the bestselling book *The Authenticity Principle*, and dedicated her life to empowering others. Most importantly, she committed to living as authentically as possible to claim belonging for herself and others.

Ritu's mission in life is to help create a more empowered, inclusive, and inspired world by unlocking belonging for all. She wants everyone to experience the magic that comes with living their truth.

Ritu still lives in Toronto but travels the world to eat, swim, dance, hike, and work.

Reach out to Ritu:
@ritu_bhasin
in/ritubhasin